Persian Springs

About Elam

Elam's mission is to strengthen and expand the church among the peoples of the Iran Region.

Elam is training and equipping Persian speakers to be leaders, preachers, and evangelists. Elam operates the only residential Bible College in the world for Persian speakers.

Elam is translating the Scriptures into Persian and other languages, and also producing literature, audio/visual materials and radio programmes.

To identify the Christian faith with compassion, Elam supports relief and development projects in the region.

About Highland Books

You can find out more from our website www.highlandbks.com where there is a downloadable catalogue. We may from time to time post emendations we find out about at www.highlandbks/errata – you are invited to e-mail errors to errata@highlandbks.com.

PERSIAN SPRINGS

PAULINE SELBY

Highland Books

First published in 2001 by Highland Books, Two
High Pines, Knoll Road, Godalming, Surrey
GU7 2EP. Reprinted 2002

ISBN: 1-897913-57-5

Printed in Great Britain by Bookmarque Limited,
Croydon.

CONTENTS

AUTHOR'S ACKNOWLEDGEMENTS

Many people were involved in the making of this book. It was Pastor Sam Yeghnazar who had the original vision for it, and I am very grateful to him for asking me to write it. I have enjoyed writing it. It has been an enriching experience, which brought me new friends and a deeper understanding of another culture.

I would also like to thank Teymour Shaheeni, who edited numerous drafts of the stories with patience as well as ruthlessness. Editing is often a thankless task, but without Teymour's efforts, this book would never have been published.

Many thanks are also due to my long-suffering family, who put up with a wife and mother who spent hours at the keyboard when she could have been cooking their meals or letting them use the computer for other purposes. They rarely complained - which I appreciated.

I am immeasurably grateful for the encouragement and prayers I received from my dear friend Claire, who continued to believe in the value of getting these stories into print, in spite of all the difficulties of the process. Other friends also read them and gave helpful comments - thank you Susan, and David. Hessam's story might never have got into this book, had it not been for the newly Christian Iranian family who gave the time to translate the original material. Some quite young members of the family were involved in this, and their contribution was greatly valued.

Finally and most important, I would like to thank Khosrow and Debby, Afarin, Dr Hedayat, and Hessam, for their willingness to share their life-stories. Through meeting them and hearing their stories, I myself have been touched and changed. I hope other people will be equally blessed, as they read this book.

I cannot forget that it was during the weekend that work on this book started - while I was staying with Khosrow and Debby in their home in Sussex, that Pastor Mohamad Yusefi was killed in the north of Iran. He had been the last surviving pastor from a Persian background to be ministering openly in Iran. It has been the example of people like him that has motivated me to keep working at this book. I hope it will make people more aware of what is happening amongst Iranians, and will generate prayer for them at this crucial time in their history.

INTRODUCTION

TOO OFTEN THE IMAGES THAT COME TO THE West from Iran are those of hatred and desire for vengeance. But these stories come from Iran – with love.

Our lives are like letters – they contain messages that are read by people we meet whether we want them to or not. I believe that the lives of these Iranian Christians are rather special letters. I see them as letters from God to the world, containing important messages not often heard these days.

The human vehicles are not perfect, so the messages they carry are not always as clear as they might be. But I pray that as people read these stories and enter into the lives of these Christians, they would hear what God wants them to hear.

These are true stories – but the names of some people and towns have been changed.

Pauline Selby   May 2000

I

KHOSROW'S STORY

"My sheep listen to my voice…and they follow me. "   (John 10:27)

The Voice of the Dove

The Voice of the Dove

A SMALL BOY WAS BEING PULLED RELUCTANTLY through the dry, dusty streets of Tehran. His mother was trying to persuade him that it was great fun to go to the barbers, but he wasn't so sure. So she tried another approach.

"There are lots of birds near the barber's shop," she said. "And you like watching birds don't you?"

The child thought about it. Yes, he did like watching birds – especially those by the barber's shop. He would go and get his hair cut – as long as he could spend some time with the birds. They were doves – his favourites.

Thirty years later, a young man and his wife and child were walking through the streets of a town in the south of England.

Suddenly the man stopped. There seemed to be a strange presence inside him that hadn't been there before, and he felt compelled to go into a shop they were passing.

So he went in – he felt he had no choice. Inside the shop, there were cards and posters as well as books. Some had pictures of doves on them.

Soon he found himself standing in front of some books that drew his attention in a special way. He took one off the shelf – it was a Bible.

———————————

Chapter One

Religion is a 'fairy story'

KHOSROW SPENT HIS EARLY YEARS IN TEHRAN, in a beautiful house that opened out onto a large courtyard. He still remembers the huge old apricot tree that grew there, and the fresh juicy sweetness of its fruit. In the middle of the yard was an ornamental fishpond with a fountain, surrounded by a low stone wall. Here people would sit and relax, enjoying the coolness and sparkle of the water. Khosrow loved water and was fascinated by that fountain.

However, garden ponds can be dangerous places for young children and there was a time when Khosrow's life nearly ended in one. He was about two years old, and his mother had gone out shopping, leaving him in the care of some older children. When she came back, they casually told her "Khosrow has fallen into the pond."

She rushed over and saw her son lying face downward in the water, apparently lifeless. The shock was too much for her and she fainted – but fortunately her sister-in-law was there, and she ran out onto the street to call for help. A man suddenly appeared who came into the garden, lifted the limp child out of the water, and revived him.

Khosrow himself has no memories of this event, but his mother told him about it when he was older. She said it was a Jewish man who had saved his life.

Khosrow's mother took her religion very seriously, and some of her son's earliest memories are of her reciting her prayers. At certain points during the prayers she would kneel and put prayer stones (tablets of baked clay), on the ground in front of her. Then she would bend forward and rest her forehead on the stones. She explained these prayer rituals to her son while he was still very small, for she wanted him to follow her example.‡ But Khosrow wasn't interested in praying – he thought it was boring. One day his mother decided to give him some extra incentive and said, "If you pray like I do, God will tell his angels to put coins under the prayer stones for you."

So he tried it and to his amazement – it worked! He did start to find coins under the prayer stones. Then one day he saw his

‡   The Islamic prayer rituals are performed several times a day. They include washing in a prescribed way, then having one's body in certain positions while reciting some set prayers, in Arabic. If any details are incorrect, the prayers are considered invalid. Other prayers can be spontaneous and in any language, but the set daily prayers have to be recited correctly, in Arabic.

mother putting the money under the stones herself, and was terribly upset. "It isn't true about the angels," he thought. "Maybe nothing is true about God and praying either."

Looking back at this incident much later, Khosrow understood his mother's good intentions, and the sincerity of her faith. But her desperate desire to make him believe what she believed had made her less than completely honest with him. It made him determined not to make the same mistake with his own children.

Another thing that troubled Khosrow about religion was the annual celebration of *Ashurah*. He came to dread that time of year, when people marched along the streets in their thousands, carrying black banners and chanting fierce-sounding slogans. His mother always took him to watch the *Ashurah* processions, as her father and his friends took an active part in them. They would carry chains or bundles of wires, which they used to beat their own backs with as they marched. After a while, the blood would start trickling down their bodies, and they seemed proud of this. But Khosrow was a gentle, sensitive boy, and the whole scene sickened him. It was a complete contrast to the beauty and peace of Persian life he experienced in his own home.

Khosrow's mother explained how the marchers were mourning for Hussein (grandson of the Prophet Mohammed), who was martyred in a battle. She said these processions were very important, to make sure that Hussein's sacrifice was not forgotten. Yet it didn't seem right to Khosrow. He decided if religion made you hit yourself till your back bled, he didn't want it.

As Khosrow grew up, other things happened to make him disillusioned with religion of any kind. The sorrow and chaos in the world upset him a lot, and he said to himself, "How can there be a God who is in control of all this mess? Different religions talk about very different gods, but they cannot all be right. How do we know which, if any is the real one?"

Khosrow's parents didn't have any other children, but he had plenty of cousins to play with. He would visit them most weekends, and in the summer they would all go on holiday together. However, when he was eleven years old, he found out that his 'cousins' were actually his brothers and sisters. And the people he called 'aunt and uncle' were in fact his 'real' parents. Khosrow was absolutely devastated by this, and wanted an explanation. So his family sat him down and told him the story.

He had been the third child of his 'real' parents, and while he was still small and needing a lot of attention, their fourth child was born. His mother was very tired at that time, so her sister and brother-in-law took him to their home for a while. This worked well until they tried to return the toddler to his own family. Every time they left him there, he screamed hysterically. Eventually it was decided that Khosrow's aunt and uncle would officially adopt him. So he had stayed in their home and grown up with them, assuming he was their own son.

Khosrow loved his aunt and uncle dearly, and knew that they loved him. He never stopped thinking of them as his parents, even after hearing the truth about his birth. But the knowledge of his adoption affected him deeply. It made him feel he'd been rejected and deceived – and these feelings stayed with him for a long time. It was all made worse by another traumatic experience he went through a few years later – which might never have happened if Iran hadn't been going through some dramatic social upheavals at that time.

It was the 1960's, when the name of Ayatollah Khomeini was not yet on everyone's lips, and the Shah of Iran (Mohammed Reza), was still very popular. These were the days when the Shah was trying to bring Iran into the modern age as quickly as possible. He was carrying out drastic land reforms, to end the old 'feudal' system of farming. He said that primary education should be compulsory for everyone, and established a 'literary corps' to provide teachers. He encouraged women to get out of their homes more, and take jobs that few women had ever done before. He invited foreign companies to bring new technology into the country, to be taught to local people. And he allowed Western style entertainment into Iran. Nightclubs and casinos, where alcohol was freely available, started to appear in Tehran, as well as dancing halls and cinemas.

For some people, this was an exciting new world and they loved it. Suddenly there were many more opportunities for young men and women to meet, and interesting places for them to go. Khosrow and his friends took advantage of the new freedoms. Films were their first interest, and as young teenagers they spent all their spare time at the cinema. Later they started meeting girls and going to dances.

However, a lot of these new activities were against Islamic law, as well as being contrary to Persian traditions.‡ Many people, especially the religious leaders, strongly opposed what the Shah was doing. So the new freedoms stayed very superficial, and in most important matters,

‡   All Islamic scholars consider that drinking alcohol and gambling are contrary to Islamic law. Some say that dancing in the presence of the opposite sex, and any music apart from a simple drumming, are also taboo. And in the old Persian traditions, young people did not meet those of the opposite sex at all, unless they were close relatives.

things did not change. For instance, although many young people started dating, the tradition of arranged marriages was still the normal practice. This caused a lot of confusion and suffering for many people – including Khosrow. For he had fallen in love – but neither he nor his girlfriend dared tell their parents.

Khosrow thought if only he could get a good job, then he might be able to marry his girlfriend. So to raise his status in the job market, he decided to try for a British qualification. His sister was already in England so she helped him apply for courses, and in 1971 he arrived in a Sussex town to study Hotel Management.

In those early days in England, Khosrow had great hopes for the future, but just six months later everything changed. He got a letter from his girlfriend, telling him that her parents had chosen another man to be her husband. They were pushing her to marry him.

Khosrow's heart sank. He wrote back at once, asking her to talk to her parents and work something out. But her reply was "I'm sorry, I can't do anything. I've got to marry this man."

This was a crushing blow to Khosrow. He had been prepared to study for several years to marry the girl he loved – but she had given him up after just six months. He knew that family pressures in Iran were very strong, but he still felt terribly hurt, and lost all sense of purpose for his future.

He was living with his sister and her husband, a German, and he poured out his heart to them. They encouraged him to stay in England and continue his studies in spite of his heartache, so he decided to do that.

Khosrow enjoyed talking with his brother-in-law. Sometimes they would sit up half the night, drinking and smoking together, discussing all sorts of things. When the question of religion came up, Khosrow was quick to express his views. "I don't think there is a God," he said. "Human nature is just weak. We want someone stronger than ourselves, to turn to when we're in trouble. So we make up fairy stories about 'gods' who can help us."

His brother-in-law disagreed. He pointed to verses from the Bible and tried to explain that Jesus was God. Khosrow was horrified. He thought if God *did* exist, He would be a distant power in heaven – unable to be seen by human beings. It was blasphemy to suggest that God had lived on earth as a man.

As well as trying to recover from a broken heart in those days, Khosrow was suffering from culture shock. It was the swinging seventies in Britain, with a growing acceptance of drugs and "free" sex.

Women wore mini-skirts and not much more, and couples had no problem kissing in the streets. It was very different from Iran, where in spite of all the changes going on, most women still dressed extremely modestly and public demonstrations of affection were taboo. Even in Tehran, where society was more Westernised, there was hardly a married couple who would as much as hold hands in public.

It wasn't easy for Khosrow to adjust to these things. He didn't want to forget his Persian upbringing, for he saw many advantages to it – and still does. Yet it was because of the Western social freedoms that he came to meet Debby – the vivacious dark-haired Jewish girl who was to become his wife.

He was living in a bedsitter in a student house by this time, and Debby lived in a flat just opposite him. He had noticed her going off to work in the mornings, and had started to admire her from afar – but he was rather shy and hadn't found a chance to speak to her.

His opportunity came one evening, when he and his sister and brother-in-law were sitting in their favourite pub on the sea front. Suddenly Debby came in with a friend of hers, and his sister turned to him and whispered, "Why don't you go and chat that girl up – it'll be good for your language."

She was pointing at Debby's friend who was an attractive blonde, but Khosrow's heart was beating faster because of the dark-haired Debby. When he saw the girls looking for cigarettes, he seized the moment and offered them some of his own. Then he bought them some drinks and they started talking. That was how it all started.

A week or so later Khosrow saw Debby again, and he asked her out. Their first date didn't go well – she didn't turn up. But he asked her out again, and soon they were going out regularly, as they both enjoyed dancing and spent a lot of time at clubs and discos. Khosrow was a slim, attractive young man with thick dark hair, and Debby enjoyed his company very much. She was a cheerful, warm-hearted girl, and Khosrow was encouraged by her friendship.

When he had nearly finished college, Khosrow asked Debby to marry him. Well he didn't actually ask her, he said, "You will marry me, won't you?" Sometimes even now, Debby laughs and says he never gave her any choice about it.

They were in love and wanted to get married, but they had a big problem – religion. Khosrow's parents were Muslims, and Debby's parents were Jewish. Khosrow and Debby didn't think religion was important, but their parents did.

It saddened the young couple to see how strongly their parents opposed their relationship, but there didn't seem to be anything they could do about it. None of their parents wanted to come to their wedding, except for Debby's mother. She was a kind lady and Khosrow became very fond of her, but tragically she died in 1976, just two years after their wedding. Khosrow and Debby missed her very much, especially as Khosrow's parents were far away in Iran, and Debby's father had never accepted Khosrow. He wouldn't even talk to him – and this hurt the young couple deeply. They were very happy together, but always in the background was the bitter fact that Debby's father wouldn't accept them. And the reason was religion.

Khosrow had already decided that religion was a 'fairy story'; now he saw it as something that tore people apart. He and Debby decided to have nothing to do with God. They made an agreement – "Religion causes problems. We don't want it ourselves, and if we have any children, we won't force it on them."

Chapter Two

Strange voices

KHOSROW HAD NEVER BEEN TEMPTED TO GAMBLE in Iran. But soon after he had arrived in England, one of his fellow students – another Iranian, had started taking him to casinos and betting shops. This had led to an obsession with gambling. Marriage made no difference – he was an addict.

However, one day a very strange thing happened – and Khosrow felt he was never quite the same person afterwards.

It was Grand National Day, a very important day for horse racing, and he wanted to put a bet on a horse. He had just sat down in his living room to study the lists of horses, when suddenly he heard a voice, talking to him. It seemed to come from inside him, and at first he thought he was imagining things. But then he thought, "No, someone IS trying to talk to me."

The voice said, "If you obey me, I will give you the name of the winning horse."

He asked "How?" and this answer came back. "Write the names of the horses on bits of paper. Screw each paper up, put them in a bowl and pick one out."

So he did it. He wrote the names of forty horses on bits of paper, screwed them up, then put them in a bowl and picked one out. He read it carefully but thought to himself, "Once isn't enough. I'll do it again."

He put the paper back, mixed them around and picked one out again. To his amazement, it was the same horse. But he still wasn't convinced, and decided to do it one more time. He put the paper back, mixed them around very thoroughly, then closed his eyes and took one out.

When he opened the paper, he could hardly believe it. It was the same horse!

Khosrow was frightened now. He didn't know what was happening.

Then he heard another voice, very different from the first voice. It said, "I will not come that way".

When he heard that second voice, Khosrow almost went to pieces. He felt he was in the presence of something "beyond himself"; something he didn't understand at all. He was very confused, and didn't bet at all that day.

Three o'clock came, and the Grand National started. Khosrow was sitting in front of the television, his eyes glued to the screen. The horse he had picked had been given odds of 12-1, so its chances didn't seem too great. Yet it wasn't long before it was thundering past the winning post – in first place.[‡]

Khosrow could hardly believe his eyes. He had thought he didn't believe in anything supernatural, but now he began to wonder.

He had not heard much about evil spirits who try to influence people in negative ways. Nor did he know about the Holy Spirit, whose symbol is a dove, who works for good in people's lives. Years later he was to hear about these things, but on that Grand National Day it was all very frightening, and he was left with a lot of unanswered questions ...

Time passed. Debby and Khosrow had a baby girl, Rebecca. Then in 1981, when Rebecca was nearly five years old, Khosrow's adoptive parents died – within a week of each other.

Khosrow went straight off to Iran, leaving Debby behind with Rebecca at a difficult time, with a lot of bills to pay. She was upset and he was upset, and when he came back to England he was still in emotional turmoil. He had loved his parents dearly, and now his mind was full of questions about life and death – "What

---

[‡]   The horse was "Red Rum" – who became a great favourite in later years but was not so well-known when Khosrow picked him out.

happens after death? Where are my parents now? Can there really be a God?"

He had once dismissed God as a fairy tale, and although the strange voices he'd heard had made him think again, they hadn't answered his questions about God. Neither had they stopped him gambling. He was continuing to gamble away his family's hard-earned money, and this was causing serious problems for him and Debby. He began to think they would be better off separated.

Khosrow got more and more desperate – till finally, in the summer of 1982 he couldn't bear it any longer. He came out of the betting shop one day, having lost a lot more money, and was overwhelmed by feelings of hopelessness. Life just wasn't worth living. He could never change his ways – he was destroying himself and his family and he couldn't stop it. He almost wished he could die.

Suddenly the events of that Grand National day came back into his mind. Again the thought came to him, "Maybe it was God who helped me not to gamble that day".

He stood still on the pavement. Not caring if anyone was watching him, he turned his face up to the sky and prayed – "If there is any God up there, I really want to know."

It was an honest prayer. He really did want to know, with all his heart.

Just one week later, Khosrow was in Brighton with Debby and Rebecca, when something very strange happened. This is how he describes it:

> We were walking along the street when suddenly I felt something in me was different. I felt controlled by something that was not me. It was really strange and it's hard to explain it – but I knew for sure that I had to go into a shop we were passing. When I looked at the sign, it said 'Christian bookshop.'
>
> I was surprised by that sign, but I went in. I had to go in – it seemed as if I had no choice. I felt very light – as if I was a different person.
>
> I found myself standing in front of some books, and felt I couldn't leave the shop without one. They were *Good News Bibles.*
>
> Debby had no idea what was happening to me. I had turned into the shop without explaining anything to her. When she saw what sort of shop it was, she couldn't understand it. I was from a Muslim background and she was Jewish – so what on earth were we doing in a Christian bookshop?
>
> I didn't understand it either – but I knew I had to buy one of those Bibles. When I got home, I couldn't wait to start reading it. There was a real thirst in me, to read that book. This was unusual for me, as I wasn't really a book-reading person.

Years earlier, when my brother-in-law had shown me verses from the Bible, I hadn't understood it at all. It had all seemed gibberish to me. But now as I read this book, I found to my amazement that I understood it. I found God bubbling up out of it – and this was wonderful.

As soon as I got home from work every day, I wanted to sit down and read that Bible. I couldn't have enough of it – I was so thirsty for it. Sometimes I read a bit before I went to work. I had so many questions, but often the questions were answered by other verses I just happened to read later.

After about nine months of reading the Bible, I came to believe there really is a God. And to my amazement, this God had always had contact with human beings. He didn't stay far apart from them, way up in the sky. No, from the very beginning, God came close to people in different ways. I had never heard these things before.

Then in the New Testament I read about Jesus – and He became like a real person to me.

My Bible-reading was very puzzling for Debby. She didn't understand it, but she noticed I was becoming a different person. I was giving up some of my bad habits, because of what I was reading in the Bible. Gambling had had a very strong hold on me, but now I didn't want to gamble any more. Jesus had become real to me and I just knew I had to stop such things.

I didn't explain all this to Debby. Maybe it was because before we'd got married, we'd told each other that religion causes problems. But maybe it wasn't that. It just never occurred to me to share with her what I was finding. Not then anyway.

By now, Khosrow had been reading the Bible for almost a year and Easter was approaching. When he saw there was going to be a film on the television about the life of Jesus, he was very excited.

Debby was going out with Rebecca that day – it was Saturday and she wanted to do some shopping. I told her I was going to stay home to watch this film – although I thought I'd know everything in it, because I'd read the book.

Yet there was one thing that still puzzled me. If God came down to earth as Jesus, to be with mankind, why did He die? Surely God is not like a man, who can die. I just couldn't accept that Jesus had died on a cross.[‡]

Anyway, I sat down that afternoon, really looking forward to watching the film. It all happened the way I knew it would. Then at the end of the film, they put a cross on the floor

[‡]   Jesus's death on the Cross is a stumbling block for many Muslims. Most Islamic scholars understand the Quran as saying that Jesus was a great prophet but He did NOT die on a cross.

and – they put Jesus on it. They put the nails in His hands and His feet.

When they lifted that cross up, it seemed that something inside me broke down. I started crying, crying like a little child. I couldn't stop myself. It felt as if a balloon of water had risen up inside me – then burst. Maybe it was love for Him, I don't know, but I was sobbing, sobbing my heart out.

I found myself shouting at the television, shouting at the man who was playing Jesus, 'If you are God, why don't you rescue yourself? Why do you allow them to kill you? Why?'

Suddenly I heard a voice – a voice I recognised. It was one of the voices I had heard on that Grand National Day – the one that had warned me against betting. Now that same voice came to me again and said, 'Son, this was for your sin.'

As soon as I heard it, it was like daylight dawning on me. Suddenly I knew why Jesus had died. The force of it put me on my knees on the floor before the television and I said, 'Jesus, You let those people kill you, for my sake. You did it because of my sin.'

One minute it had been a big puzzle to me – the next minute I could see it as clear as anything. Jesus had taken the punishment that I deserved for my sins, upon Himself. That's why He had died. I really accepted Him into my life at that point. Yes, that's how I became a Christian.

Chapter Three

The Voice that Leads

KHOSROW NOW WANTED TO GO TO A CHURCH, but although he tried several different churches, he didn't feel at home in any of them. He had a great thirst for God, but every time he went to a church service he came out feeling dry and unsatisfied.

Someone else was having similar problems with churches in those days, and he lived very near Khosrow and Debby. Khosrow noticed the old man as he was walking back from the shops one day, for he looked breathless and kept stopping to rest. Khosrow thought he might be ill, so he asked him if he needed any help. He said he was all right, but then they started to talk.

The old man's name was Mr. Quibel – an unusual name for an unusual character. His conversation was full of phrases like 'God willing', which interested Khosrow so he asked, "Mr. Quibel, are you a Christian?" ‡

---

‡   Mr. Quibel was aware that many people call themselves Christians, without it meaning much to them. The word 'Christian' is hardly used in the Bible, and Jesus never used it. He talked about people needing to be 'born again' or 'born of the Spirit' if they are to enter the Kingdom of God.

"A Christian – what do you mean by that? Yes, I am born again."

"Alleluia!" said Khosrow. "I think I am born again too."

That was the beginning of a beautiful friendship. They walked on up the street together, and had a lot to talk about. It was a great day for Khosrow, for he felt that God had given him a spiritual father, to nurture him. Khosrow was in his thirties, and Mr. Quibel was over eighty years old.

Earlier in his life, Mr. Quibel had been a keen communist. Then a worker at his factory had given him a tract about Jesus, and he read it and accepted Jesus into his life. It hadn't been through any human persuasion; it had been through something he read by himself. Khosrow could identify with that.

Mr. Quibel had a small group of friends who met to worship God in their own homes, so Khosrow started to join them. This was his first experience of Christian fellowship, and he loved it. There were only five or six of them, but they had a great time singing and praying together, and studying the Bible.

Khosrow was keen to learn all he could from the Bible. One day he read that God says, "Your body is My temple" – and that hit him hard. He thought, "If my body is God's temple, why am I spoiling it by smoking and drinking?" So he prayed,

"Lord, I don't want to destroy my body. Help me to keep it clean."

The next morning when he found a few cigarettes in his pocket, he threw them away – and never smoked another cigarette again. He had never been a chain smoker, but giving up cigarettes still made a big difference to his lifestyle.

As Khosrow studied more of the Bible, he believed it was God's will for him to be baptised. His original plan was to be baptised in the sea by Mr. Quibel, but the water was too cold for the old man. Eventually some friends arranged for him to join in a baptism service at their church in London, where there was a warm pool. So many people wanted to go – including Debby and her sister and Khosrow's mother – that they had to hire a minibus to get everyone there.

Khosrow still remembers how significant it felt to be baptised 'in the Name of the Father, the Son, and the Holy Spirit'. Before his baptism, he hadn't felt comfortable about calling God his Father. Now that was not a problem – talking to God as Father felt very natural. It also seemed a very precious privilege, and he kept wanting to thank God for it.[‡] At last that sense of rejection that had gone so deep in him, began to fade away.

The year after Khosrow was baptised, Khosrow and Debby had another baby – a son. They called him Joel and dedicated him to God. Joel was a happy, healthy child, but when he was eighteen months old he nearly died – on a shopping trip that turned into a nightmare.

It was a cold spring day in 1987, and Debby had wrapped her toddler up in a warm fleecy baby suit. Then they all went out shopping. Khosrow continues:

> Suddenly I looked down at Joel in the buggy and knew something was wrong. He wasn't breathing properly, and his eyes were turned up in a very strange way. I picked him up and shouted at Debby, 'Run to the car! He's not breathing! We've got to get him to the hospital.'
>
> She started crying and I said, 'Just pick up the buggy and run after me. Don't cry, you can cry later.'
>
> So we ran to the car. I had Joel on my shoulder and from time to time I pressed him on his back. I was trying to start him breathing again.

---

‡   For someone from Khosrow's background this was very significant. In Iranian culture, the concept of 'Father' usually refers to a blood relationship, and is not used to describe a spiritual/emotional relationship.

Sometimes he made a little gasping noise, but then he would go silent.

When we got to the car, I put Debby and Joel into the back and drove off as fast as I dared. As we were going along the road by the sea, I was desperately praying – 'Lord, help us. You have given us this child – I have dedicated him to You. If You want to take him, take him, but what is the point?'

Suddenly the Lord was there. I heard His voice and He said, 'Turn left.'

I knew the hospital was straight ahead – turning left would take us away from it. So I argued with the Lord and said, 'Why turn left? The hospital is straight ahead.'

Again I heard the voice saying 'Turn left.'

So I turned left – I couldn't resist that voice. As soon as I turned, I realised that the Children's Hospital was at the end of that road. I had been going to the Royal Sussex Hospital, but the Children's was nearer, and a much better place to take a child.

I said 'Thank you Lord, thank you Lord.'

When we got to the hospital, they hurried Joel away to another room, and closed the door on us. I knelt down on a bench and poured my heart out before the Lord. I said, 'Lord, again I'm telling You – if You want to take him, take him. But You gave him to us after I came to know You. He is already Yours...'

I talked on and on like this, but I didn't really know what I was saying.

After a while the doctors came out and said, 'He's breathing now, you can go and see him. But wait a minute – I need to prepare you for something. Your son wasn't breathing properly for at least fifteen minutes. He may have suffered brain damage.'

The doctor explained that children under three can't control their body temperature very well. They easily get over-heated and suffer convulsions. That's what had happened to Joel.

I told the doctor, 'I believe in a God, a God who is above all other Gods. It's all up to Him'.

The doctor just looked at me, then went away.

Joel stayed in the hospital for a few days, then had to return for follow-up visits for several months. They did lots of tests on him, but all the results were OK. Finally they told us, "Nothing is wrong with this child".

I'm sure if I hadn't taken Joel straight to the Children's Hospital when he collapsed, he would have died or suffered brain damage. God did a miracle for us that day.

Whenever Khosrow speaks of that incident, he has to hold back his tears.

Joel's 'miracle' reminded Khosrow of his own miraculous escape from death, when he had been a toddler drowning in a garden pond. His mother had told him it was a Jewish man who'd saved his life that day, and he often wondered how she'd known the man had been Jewish. Then later in his life something very unexpected happened, that shed more light on the matter...

I had gone to bed one night when I felt the Lord say, 'Go downstairs and worship Me.' So I went down and worshipped Him. It was a wonderful time, when Jesus seemed very close. I felt completely caught up in love and praise for Him.

Then a picture came into my mind. To my surprise I was looking down at a fishpond in a courtyard – like I was hovering up in the air above it. I could see a child floating face down in the water, looking as if he was dead. Then I saw a man come along and lift him out, hold him upside down and shake him. Water gushed out of the child's mouth, then the man slapped on his back and he started breathing again.

I tried to move to a different part of the picture in my mind, so that I could see the man's face. But I couldn't do it. Then I heard a voice saying, 'Don't try to see his face. He is an angel that I sent'.

The incident in the fishpond wasn't the only time that Khosrow nearly drowned. When he was a teenager, he had been playing on an inflatable raft in the sea when the raft drifted far out from the shore – and he couldn't swim.

After some very anxious hours, a friend of his father managed to rescue him.‡

As time passed, Khosrow experienced more dramatic incidents of God guiding him – but it wasn't always as clear as it had been in the early days. Some of his most fervent prayers were not answered in the ways he longed for, and sometimes life seemed a great struggle. Occasionally doubts and negative thoughts seemed to overwhelm him, and at first he couldn't understand this. Later he decided, "Well I'm sure these terrible thoughts are not from me, and they cannot be from the Lord. So they must be from Satan.*

These struggles drove Khosrow to prayer more and more, and he gradually learnt more about the harsh spiritual battles going on in this world. Khosrow realised that amongst all the different thoughts that came into his mind, he needed to recognise the voice of God's Holy Spirit – the voice of the dove.

‡ Khosrow's enjoyment of water wasn't put off by those near disasters. He still loves walking by the sea – and he still enjoys fish ponds. He has made one for himself in his garden in Sussex – where he also keeps pigeons and doves...

* The Bible talks a lot about Satan (the devil). It describes him as an evil spiritual being who tries to deceive people and make them do wrong.

Chapter Four

The Voice that tells others

AS HE GREW STRONGER IN HIS FAITH, KHOSROW longed to share his discoveries about God with other people. But he didn't find this easy, and for a long time the person closest to him – Debby – was the hardest one to share with. She didn't object to his belief in Jesus, for she thought it had changed him for the better. She was even happy to have Mr. Quibel's meetings in her house, and to make tea and biscuits for the visitors. But that was as far as it went – until one day something happened that touched her deeply. She explains:

> I'd been serving tea for people at the meeting and was back in the kitchen, puffing at a cigarette. Then I heard this *beautiful* voice, singing. It really was heavenly – like something out of this world. It made my hair stand on end.

> I didn't want to go in and disturb them, but I wanted to know who was singing like that. So I went quietly up to the door and put my head round to see. Khosrow still remembers me creeping into that room with a plate and tea towel in my hand. He says I was staring at Lesley – who was singing – with my eyes wide open in amazement.

Lesley's singing touched me so much, that I began to sit in on the meetings sometimes. But I didn't think I'd ever become a Christian, because I was Jewish. In my mind, Jews just didn't become Christians.

However, things changed when a Messianic fellowship (Jewish Christian Fellowship) started in their town. This is how Debby describes it.

Khosrow kept telling me that Jesus was the Jewish Messiah, but I didn't listen to him. Then we heard about the Messianic Fellowship, and he was very pleased about that. He thought I might listen to Jews who believed in Jesus, even if I didn't listen to him.

Eventually I decided I would visit this fellowship, to see what it was like. I really liked the atmosphere, so I started going quite often. At the end of their meetings, they would invite people up to the front for prayer. One day I felt I wanted prayer too – so I went up. Khosrow came with me. The pastor said if I felt the Lord was working in me, I could repeat a prayer after him. It was the 'sinner's prayer' accepting Jesus into my heart as my Saviour.[‡] Suddenly Khosrow saw that I was shaking like a leaf, and was repeating the prayer after the man.

‡ The "sinner's prayer" is a prayer in which a person admits they are always coming short of God's standards. They say they are sorry, and accept Jesus as their Saviour. They then trust that their sins are forgiven, because Jesus died to pay the punishment for their sins.

Things have been different since then. One thing was that I had a different attitude to my father. I was able to forgive him for the past, and show him more love and respect. When he was ill, I went to see him in hospital and things got a lot better between us. I think he noticed the difference in me, even if he didn't say so.

I look forward to going to church now, instead of just thinking I ought to go. I've met other Jewish people who have accepted Jesus, and I always feel a special link with them. We're Christians but we're still Jewish, and that's very precious to us.

Debby's Jewishness is also precious to Khosrow. He feels that it links him in a special way to the people of the Bible – and he hasn't forgotten it was a Jewish man who saved his life when he was a child.

———————

Mr. Quibel was already an old man when Khosrow first met him, yet it seemed God gave him an extra few years of strength, so he could help others grow in their faith. Having done that, he died. Khosrow missed him terribly. The people in Mr. Quibel's group gradually went off to other churches, and at first Khosrow felt he had lost everything. Then a friend of his told him there was an Iranian church in London. He'd seen the address in a phone book, and noted it down.

Khosrow was surprised, and very interested. He wanted to know if there were any *Persian* Christians in this church, for although some of his school friends in Tehran had been Christians, they had been Armenians, not Persians.[‡] He had never met another Persian Christian, and had begun to think he was the only one.

One Sunday morning he drove to London and found his way to the Iranian church. People were very friendly, and he instantly felt at home there. First he met some English people, then he met the Armenian pastor, and then he met some Persians from backgrounds like his own. As he talked with them, he soon realised what a vibrant and joyful faith they had in Jesus. He was thrilled.

Khosrow started going regularly to the Iranian church, and sometimes took Debby and the children with him. The church was in London, over an hour's journey from their home, but that did not stop him. He felt that God was telling him, "This is the place for you. Stay and work for me here."

So that's what he did...

At first, Khosrow didn't talk to people very much about his faith. He is a quiet, rather shy person, and it didn't come easily

[‡]   There are over 100,000 Armenians in Iran and practically all belong to the Armenian Orthodox Church. They were first brought in by King Shah Abbas in the 16th century.

to him. Yet as time passed, he found his confidence growing. He began to get great satisfaction from telling people about his adventures with God. People at the Iranian church soon recognised his gifts, and he was given more responsibility there. One of his main roles became that of welcoming newcomers to the church, and talking to them about Jesus.

Over the years, many people have been helped to believe in Jesus, through Khosrow's ministry. One was a lady called Vida (not her real name) who was seeking God, but was confused about all the different religions. Khosrow talked with her after church one day.

I asked Vida why she'd come to church, and what she thought about Jesus. She didn't really know, so I told her that Jesus is the only way to God. I like to be direct with people – then I can find out where they're at, and go on from there.

Vida was interested in what I said, but wasn't sure if it was really true. She came back to church the next week and we went on discussing things. But after I'd talked to her several times, I told her, 'I can't help you any more. You have to ask God to show you the truth about Jesus. I'm sure He will one day.'

She kept on coming to church and I kept asking her, 'Vida, is this the day God is showing you the truth?' Her reply was always, 'No. Nothing's happening today.'

Then one Sunday I was sitting near the front of the church, when suddenly I thought, 'Someone behind me needs help.' I turned round and saw Vida sitting a few rows behind me. I felt the Lord was telling me, 'Today is the day for Vida.'

So I went and sat beside her. I started praying and she started crying. I put my hand on her shoulder and said, 'Vida, why are you crying? Is today the day?' She nodded then said, 'Yes, the Lord is talking to me. Now I know it's true about Jesus.'

So I took her to the front, and Brother Sam prayed for her. Afterwards she came over to me and said, 'How did you know I needed help at that moment? I was just sitting there praying to God to show me the truth. Suddenly I felt your hand on me.'

I said, 'God told me that somebody behind me needed prayer. When I turned round I could only see you. Everyone else faded away. So I knew today was the day for you.'

Vida still comes to the church. She brings her mother along too, these days.

It isn't always easy to talk about Jesus, in English society. But it is even harder in Iran, where since the Islamic revolution, many Christians from Muslim backgrounds and even simple enquirers have been arrested, interrogated and threatened with dire consequences if they continue in the Christian faith. Some have ignored the warnings and been tortured – seven church leaders have been killed.‡

Khosrow wept over these martyrdoms, as did many other people. He was shocked to realise the terribly high price being paid in his homeland, for sharing the Christian message with others. But it made him think more about the preciousness of his faith, and inspired him to keep following his Lord, whatever the cost.

Khosrow believes that sharing about Jesus with other Persians is one of God's special plans for his own life. He explains:

I talk to anyone about my faith – but Persians are more open to the message of Jesus when it comes from me, than when it comes from people from other backgrounds.

I used to think I was the only Persian Christian in the world, but in the years since the revolution, more Iranians have accepted Jesus Christ as their Saviour than ever before. It is happening all over the world. I believe these are special days in the history of Iran. God is

‡   These martyrs are Rev. Arastoo Syah (pastor of the Anglican church in Shiraz, murdered in 1979), Bahram Dehqani-Tafti (son of the Episcopelian Bishop, murdered in 1980), Rev.Hussein Soodemand (pastor of Pentecostal church in Mashhad, hanged in prison in 1990), Rev. Haik Hovsepian Mehr (head of Pentecostal church, murdered in 1994), Rev. Tateos Michaelian (head of Presbyterian church, murdered in 1994), Rev. Mehdi Dibaj (Pentecostal pastor murdered in 1994 after 9 years in prison), Rev. Mohamad Yusefi (Pentecostal pastor murdered in 1996).

blessing us in new ways, and wants to bless others through us.

We have such a precious faith. Most people don't know what will happen when they die, but we know we are going to heaven. Our salvation is through Jesus – not through our own goodness. That's the most important truth in the world.

But people need to hear the truth. Sometimes I wish I could shout this message to everyone on the streets: **'Wake up people… God is a loving God... Open your eyes and see what Jesus has done for you'.**

Khosrow never tires of telling people about Jesus, for he has never lost his sense of wonder at what Jesus has done for him. He still remembers the day he knelt by his television in tears – crying out to God – desperate to know why Jesus had been killed. He cannot forget the voice that replied, 'Son, this was for your sin'.

Fifteen years have now passed since Khosrow accepted Jesus into his life. He has become a little more stout and balding (his own words), but this adds to his mature, fatherly look. His gentle face seems to shine out a sense of peace, and he has a kind, friendly manner that is very disarming. Newcomers to the church soon feel at ease when he comes to welcome them. His opportunities to serve God have increased over the years. He helps to teach new believers and prepare them for baptism. He has led teams of Bible college students on missions to other cities. He has stood up in a crowded smoky café where people in a run-down area of town get free meals, and has told them all about the love of Jesus. Some laughed at him on that occasion, but others came up and hugged him, with tears in their eyes.

A lot has happened in the life of the little Persian boy who was once dragged reluctantly through the streets of Tehran to the barber's shop. The boy saw a flock of doves that day, and was attracted to them. Maybe his response to those birds was a tiny picture of what was to come – a lifetime of responding to the Holy Spirit of God.

II

HESSAM'S STORY

"Ask and it will be given to you; seek and
you will find; knock and the door will be
opened to you..." (Matthew 7:7)

A Book under a Bed

A Book under a Bed

THERE WAS A THIN LAYER OF SNOW COVERING the ground, as the young man walked slowly along the street. His head was bowed, for he was desperately searching the gutters for cigarette ends. He was shivering with cold, but whenever he saw a bit of cigarette he would pick it out of the snow, give it a shake, and stuff it into his pocket. Later he went back to his room, to dry his findings out over the radiator.

One night there were no cigarette ends to be found. In angry frustration, he went up to a vending machine and smashed the side in...

Hessam is now a dignified young man with a quiet, serious manner. He usually has a calm, steady expression on his face, which gives no indication of the turmoils he went through in his earlier life. This is his story, in his own words.

Chapter One

A respected family

WHEN I THINK BACK OVER MY EARLY LIFE, there are a lot of things that make me feel sad. But I want to write about it, so people will understand how my life changed.

I was born in a small town in central Iran. Most of the people were very strict Muslims, but our family was not very religious. Our womenfolk always wore the veil when they went out, as did all the women in our town, but I don't remember anyone praying and fasting in our household. We had a Quran that was kept up on a shelf, but it was never read. Yet people respected us. My uncle was a famous lawyer and my father ran a big pharmacy store. The street we lived in was named after us.

It had been my grandfather who first established the pharmacy. He'd been an expert in herbal medicines and was also a Muslim clergyman and a poet. Later in my life, I also became interested in religion and writing, but it was the pharmacy that interested me first. When my father took over the daily running of it, I would often go to the store with him, and try and make myself useful. I would learn the names of the drugs, and help him read the doctor's handwriting on the prescriptions.

I enjoyed spending time with my father, but he was a bit distant and we never got to know each other very well. I still regret that. I wanted to be closer to him, but he had his own friends and was out of the house a lot.

There were eight of us children in our family – four girls and four boys, and I was the youngest. My father didn't spend much time with us, but my mother was always there. She was the backbone of our family – very kind, always ready to listen.

My mother was not from our town – she came from Shiraz. My father married her and brought her to our town when she was about sixteen, before she had finished her schooling. Her family had not wanted her to get married so soon, but she had wanted it and I think she was happy with my father. However, life wasn't easy for her. Her first child, a little girl, died when she was only four years old. My mother grieved very deeply over this, especially as the little girl died of a common childhood disease which wasn't considered to be serious. She never forgot that first child, but she kept going and gave her love and attention to her other children.

Like all families, we had our set routines and nothing much seemed to change over the years. Sometimes we children wished something different would happen, to make life more exciting. But when things did happen, it was extremely painful.

The first painful thing was that a cousin of ours killed himself.

This cousin and his family lived next door to us – and we could see into their garden from our roof. People in Iran use their flat roofs like little courtyards, and I enjoyed spending time on ours. It was a relaxing place to be – pleasantly cool in the summer evenings.

One summer I noticed that this cousin was spending a lot of time in his garden, but he didn't look happy. He kept walking round in circles, smoking constantly. I was told he suffered from depression, and was very sick.

Then one day we heard terrible screaming coming from our uncle's house. We hurried round, only to find out that our cousin was dead. He had taken an overdose of sleeping tablets and by the time his family found him, it was too late to save him. I couldn't understand this at all. I asked myself, "Why should anyone want to kill himself? We're all so afraid of dying – most of us fight as hard as we can to stay alive. Can there be anything better than this life, after death?"

These were important questions to me – but no one could give me any satisfactory answers.

Not long after my cousin's death, my father became ill. He tried to cover it up and pretended there was nothing wrong with him, but he gradually got worse. One night my mother was so worried that she took him to the hospital, and they kept him there for several days. When he came home, the doctors said he needed a complete rest. He was given a special diet, and there were many things he couldn't eat or drink.

One thing he could drink was fresh orange juice, and it became my job to make it for him. I mixed it in a blender that we'd bought specially, and took it to his bedside after lunch every day. I was fourteen years old, and enjoyed having that responsibility. I would often sit with him while he drank it, and felt those times brought us closer to each other.

When my father had finished his orange juice, he would have a sleep. He always had a sleep in the afternoons, even before he was ill. He used to tell me that afternoon sleep was very special, and he didn't want to be disturbed during it.

One afternoon I took my father his orange juice as usual, but he said he was tired, and would drink it later. I had a test at school the next day, so I didn't stay with him. I took my books and went into the garden to study, as it was too hot to concentrate indoors.

My mother and sisters had gone out shopping, so my father was alone in the house. At one point I went back in to see him, but he was fast asleep. I noticed he hadn't drunk his orange juice, and wondered whether to wake him and remind him of it. But I didn't want to disturb him. When my mother and sister came back later, I said "Father is asleep, but he didn't drink his orange juice."

A few minutes later I heard shouting and screaming. Everyone was rushing around hysterically, and soon I realised what had happened. Our father had died – while he was all alone.

I went to my room and cried. I went on crying all day and all night – I couldn't get to sleep. I kept asking myself "Why should this happen, just as I was getting to know my father better? I wanted us to go places together, to be proud of each other. Now it's all over."

The last words I had spoken about him kept echoing round my head: "Father is asleep, but he didn't drink his orange juice."

I wondered what time he had actually passed away, and whether there was anything I could have done to help him. No one blamed me, but I still wondered ...

Even now, I regret not having had a closer relationship with my father. After his death I felt like someone who was always looking for something, but never finding it. A friend of mine told me I was trying to find another father figure. Maybe I was.

A couple of years later, the revolution came to Iran. Things happened then, that made me glad my father was not around.

In all the years I'd been growing up, our family had been greatly respected in our town, for we were well educated and prosperous. However, after the revolution this all changed, for we weren't very religious, and people thought we were supporters of the Shah. First they changed the name of our street – it was no longer named after us. Many street names in Iran were being changed at that time, and anything that was considered to be pro-Shah or not suitably Islamic, had to go.

Then our uncle's office was broken into. He was a lawyer, and all his belongings were stolen or thrown out into the street, and they set fire to it all. One of my brothers saw what was happening and we ran round to help put out the fire. It was too late to save the office, but at least we were able to stop the fire spreading to other buildings.

Not long after that, I smelt burning again and went up onto our roof to see what was happening. It was evening time and I could see flames lighting up the sky, coming from another house on our street. It made me feel sick. I knew that house belonged to us – we had rented it out to a government forestry organisation, and they had an office there. All government offices were being targeted in those days. People took what was useful, then burnt them down.

There was nothing we could do to save that forestry office, so we didn't try. It wasn't worth the risk. People didn't respect us any more, and some would spit and insult us as we walked by. I was so glad that my father didn't have to experience that.

We were afraid that people would burn our pharmacy next. After my father had died I was working there more often, and would sometimes do an evening shift, staying till quite late at night. Sometimes people came to the pharmacy in a very agitated state, demanding tranquilizers and anti-depressants. We couldn't always supply these as they were in short supply after the revolution, but people didn't always understand this. Sometimes they got angry with us, and this frightened me, especially when I was there in the evenings. I was only sixteen or seventeen, and was afraid people might actually attack me or the pharmacy. But they never did, and we thanked God for that.

When I left school in 1980, I felt I wanted a change from life in my home town.

It seemed a small and boring place – I wanted to see more of the world. So I set my heart on going to Tehran and studying to be a doctor. However, at that time all the universities were closed, while they changed the education system to make it in line with Islamic principles. So for the next two years I did my military service, near the Persian Gulf.

After I'd completed my military service, the universities had opened again so I applied to study medicine. However, although I passed the entrance exam, I wasn't given a place at the medical college. At first I didn't understand what had happened. Later I discovered someone had told the college authorities that my family didn't have the correct religious attitudes to life. So, my hopes and dreams of becoming a doctor were crushed.

I tried to pretend this didn't bother me, but it made me very bitter and angry. When I was alone, I cried. I thought how easy it had been, for a few selfish people to speak some casual words and ruin my life.

Soon my anger turned to despair, and I began to think there was no hope for me. I thought I'd never be able to get a good education, or make much of my life. I thought of my poor cousin who'd committed suicide – realising how he must have lost all hope like I had. It was a terrible feeling.

Chapter Two

Books are better than people

THERE WAS SO MUCH BITTERNESS IN ME IN THOSE days, that people didn't enjoy my company very much. I didn't enjoy theirs either, so I started reading books – especially biographies. I decided that books were better company than people. They give a lot without demanding anything in return.

I had an old school friend called Nader, who kept in touch with me through that difficult time. He was a keen reader like me, and he wrote a lot of poems. I enjoyed his poems and he encouraged me to write things too. I wasn't good at poetry, so instead I started writing short stories. Nader and I would assess each other's work, and encourage each other.

When I'd been a child, I'd never been any good at writing. I'd always asked my mother to help me with my essays, so when we had exams I had big problems and sometimes cheated. Then I won first prize in a school essay competition (without my mother's help), and that was a turning point for me. I'd been afraid to take part in that competition, and had nearly gone home saying I was ill. But I was ashamed to lose face in front of my friends, so I had stayed. Later I was amazed when they announced my name as the winner. After that, I stopped asking my mother for help with writing.

In spite of that poor start, writing had now become the driving force in my life. I began to dream of being a famous writer...

Yet my writing was never cheerful. There had been a lot of discouragement and sadness in my life, so my characters were like that too. Things always went wrong for them and they usually ended up in the grave, having had no real purpose in their lives. I think my message was that whether things go well for us or not, we just have to accept it – we have no choice.

Some people told me they liked my stories. They said they made them cry. No one questioned why they were always so sad, and the new generation in Iran seemed able to relate to my characters.

Writing was a hobby, but I still wanted to do something more practical with my life, so I offered my services as a volunteer in a social services organisation. They were suspicious of me at first, because of my background, but then they accepted me and I was sent to work in some villages. We arranged food distribution, as well as helping to dig water channels. It was hard work, but I enjoyed it.

These villages were very poor, but I was impressed by the people there. They had to struggle to survive, but they seemed honest and cheerful. I was upset that they had such a hard life, through no fault of their own. Up to then, God hadn't played much role in my life, but now I wanted to complain to Him about the unfairness of life. It was unfair for these village folk, and it had been unfair to me too.

But I didn't feel right about complaining to God – He might get angry with me.

I had always thought of God as being angry and disapproving. I thought you had to obey a lot of strict rules to make God approve of you and it seemed so impossible, that I had never tried it. God was far too hard to please. He certainly didn't seem to want people to enjoy life.

Yet the people I was working with seemed to be enjoying life, and believed they were serving God. They got their ideology from Islam, and were helping other people and were thankful for everything. I respected them for that, so I decided I'd try and follow their example and be more religious myself.

I started to say my daily prayers, and went to meetings where the Quran was read. I found myself a *guru*, a spiritual leader whom I could follow absolutely, without question. I bought all this man's books as well as other religious books, and tried to study them all. But none of these things satisfied me. I didn't find answers to the questions that were in my mind, and didn't find any peace with God through it all.

Gradually I came to believe that religion had no power to help people change at heart.

My family wanted me to try for university again, for now I'd done some social work I might have more chance of being accepted. But I'd lost interest in further education. I felt that my country was not interested in people like me – they just wanted those with high Islamic ideals. I began to feel more and more lost as a person, as I had no faith in religion, or in life generally.

My poet friend Nader understood me. One day he said he would take me to meet someone very interesting, who would cheer me up. He didn't tell me much about this person – just that they liked literature and poetry and I was sure to like them. I thought he was going to introduce me to a pretty girl – maybe one who had read some of my stories. So I went along very happily.

He took me to a shop and when we got inside, I saw someone sitting behind a desk. It wasn't a pretty girl as I had hoped – it was an old man. He was about seventy years old, rather bald and wearing a pair of thick glasses. At first glance he looked rather ordinary, but soon he was to become very special to me.

This wasn't the first time he and I had met. He had a daughter called Parveen who was about my age, and when we were children we used to play together. Sometimes I had gone round to their house to play, but when we started to grow up, our parents had stopped this. Nowadays when I saw Parveen in the street, we would say "hello" as we passed, but that was all. She had become very beautiful, and boys used to talk about her.

Anyway, now I was facing Parveen's father again, in a dusty shop. He looked at me with interest and said, "You remind me of someone, young man." I wasn't sure what he was thinking, so I didn't say anything. He may have remembered me very well, but neither of us mentioned it – we went on to talk about other things.

After that first meeting, Nader and I often went back to Parveen's father's shop. It sold garden equipment but that wasn't our special interest – it was the old man himself. He was interested in poetry and books, like we were. He used to tell us a lot of stories, and I enjoyed listening to him. He was encouraged by that, and said it was good to meet a young man who would listen. We called him *Ostad* which is a respectful word meaning 'teacher'.

Although Ostad was a serious sort of man, he also told us jokes and made us laugh. We knew that he liked us, and we liked him too. He didn't look down on us because we were young. He was always a very calm person, which impressed us. Even when his shop was robbed one day, he didn't seem too upset. A lot of money had gone, but he said it didn't matter. He was more bothered about the mess the thieves had made, and how he would get his files back into order.

Ostad had high moral values and would often talk to me about the right and wrong things in life. He treated me like a son in some ways, and I thought of him like a father. But I was very disappointed when he told me he'd spent years looking for a purpose in life, and hadn't really found one. I remember him saying, "If I haven't found any purpose in all those years, how can you expect to?"

I found that very depressing, and told him so. He sympathised, but said that life is full of disappointments. If we are prepared for that, it helps us cope with it. He also said it wasn't worth fighting for great luxury in one's life. He was a rich man himself, but believed that one happy moment with friends, free from lies and hypocrisy, was worth far more than the material luxuries in life that we struggle for.

I respected Ostad very much, and his words had a deep effect on me – even though I didn't act on them much at that time.

Although Ostad had several children, he admitted that he was lonely, and tired of life. He felt that he had started life alone, and was finishing it alone. He was usually a cheerful person and laughed and joked with us – but once he had said those things, I knew how he felt deep down.

Soon after that, I left my home town and went to Tehran. I was tired of small town life, and wanted to see something of the big city. To earn a living, I got a job in a baker's office, and lost touch with Ostad and Nader. I didn't find anyone like them in Tehran, which was a pity. Then out of the blue, I got a letter from Nader. This is what he said:

Dear Hessam,

I'm afraid I have bad news – about Ostad. Soon after you left, he became ill, and I noticed how thin he looked. He would wear his usual clothes, but they all looked too big for him –even his hat. When I went into his shop he would welcome me with a smile and ask after you, but although he would still joke with me about things, I sensed he was in pain.

I remember seeing him out on the street once, walking along very slowly. He was going over the bridge, wearing his old green hat and a long coat. I waved at him and he saw me, but he didn't wave back. I felt he wanted to be alone.

After a while I heard that he was in hospital. I meant to go and see him, but somehow I didn't find time. Then I heard that he'd passed away.

Lots of people came to his funeral – they came from many different places. But where were those people when he was alive?

When I read Nader's letter I cried and cried, but it didn't comfort me. Whenever I thought about Ostad's death I had a terrible sinking feeling. I felt as if I had lost my father again, but Ostad hadn't just been like a father – he had been a friend.

I felt bereft, and even more disappointed with life.

Chapter Three

Losing our souls

I LIVED IN TEHRAN FOR TWO YEARS, BUT CITY life didn't do me much good. I lost all my high ideals of working hard and helping people, and didn't find any other purpose in life. For some reason I felt I needed to be a completely different person – and didn't feel it could happen while I was in Iran.

Lots of people were disillusioned with life in Iran after the revolution, and they wanted to find new lives for themselves in the West. So that's what I decided to do. I decided I would fly to Germany on a tourist visa, then ask for refugee status. I worked out a false story to tell to the German authorities, and hoped they would believe me.

My plan seemed to work at first. I got to Germany, told my story, and was sent to a hostel where refugees stayed until their cases were investigated. However, the hostel was in a small, isolated town in Southern Germany, where many elderly people went to retire. They wanted to live the last years of their lives in peace and quiet. We were energetic young people who had come out of difficult situations, bringing our own problems with us.

You can imagine the stress of the situation. We asylum seekers were not allowed to do any paid work, and not allowed to travel further than thirty kilometres from the town. There was no variety in our lives, and the hostel was very crowded, with six or seven people sleeping in each room. People were from different countries, with different customs, and we didn't get on well. Almost every day there would be fights between us – sometimes violent ones.

We had to stay in the hostel until our cases were heard in the courts, which usually took about two years. After that, some of us would be given residency in Germany but some would be sent back to their own countries. This was like a sword hanging over us, for we knew if we went back to our own countries, our situation would be even worse than before.

The longer I lived at that hostel, the worse my character became. I started to smoke and drink alcohol, which made me feel better for a while, but not for long. Out of boredom, I started stealing from shops and vandalising vending machines. I didn't even feel guilty about it.

Sometimes we got jobs as casual labourers on farms, and this helped a bit.

But then we were discovered and arrested by the police. We had to sign a paper saying we wouldn't work illegally any more.

The police came to know us very well – most of us were in trouble for one thing or another. We were always shoplifting, and whenever we went into a shop, we'd notice the owners watching us very carefully. We didn't look German, so they knew we were from the hostel. Whenever anything went wrong in the town, the police were at our doors checking on us. Sometimes it wasn't our fault – but usually it was.

I knew I was sinking lower and lower, but didn't seem able to do anything about it. I remember one night when I desperately wanted to smoke but didn't have any money. I went out in the street, even though there was snow on the ground, and walked around collecting cigarette ends. I was shivering with cold, but I picked the cigarette ends out of the snow and went back to the hostel. Then I dried them out on the radiators and made them into more cigarettes.

As I looked at those dirty old cigarette ends, memories of my past came back to me. I remembered my father, and how proud he had been when I did well at school. I remembered the kindly Ostad, and his high moral standards of life. I remembered the village where I had worked so hard, trying to get people a water supply.

"What have I become?" I asked myself

It seemed that we hostel dwellers were somehow losing our souls. We didn't know who we were any more. We'd lost our sense of identity with our homelands, and any standards we'd been brought up with. We'd lost our pride and self-respect, and our sense of value as human beings. Even our hope for the future seemed to be snuffed out. One man committed suicide. Another went berserk and was sent to a mental hospital. Many were taking illegal drugs. I was addicted to cigarettes and alcohol, and spent most of my time lounging around in bed, or drunk, or chatting up Polish girls.

I never thought I could fall so low, but as time went by, I went even lower. I felt as if I was going deeper into dirtiness, and couldn't stop myself. I wasn't even trying to stop myself – I had no interest in doing anything at all. I even wondered if I was going mad.

One day I started talking to a spider in a web in a corner of my room. It became a part of my life to share things with this little creature. I even caught flies for him, and put them into his web... As I watched the spider build more webs and extend his territory, it seemed that he was getting richer and fatter, and I was getting poorer and thinner. I felt miserable, stuck in a situation I couldn't improve or escape from. Not so the spider. He worked hard and was getting somewhere.

Eventually my application for asylum came before the courts. I went for my all important interview, and told them a load of lies. Well it wasn't all lies, it was a mixture of reality and imagination – but a few weeks later I was told that my application had been rejected.

You might imagine that after that, any spark of hope would have been snuffed out of me. But sometimes things happen that we don't expect.

Chapter Four

The Book Under The Bed

I DECIDED TO APPEAL AGAINST MY REJECTION for asylum. I knew it would take two years for my appeal to be heard – which meant more dreary time at the hostel, but I was desperate not to go back to Iran.

However, not long after that our supervisors made an unexpected visit, and said they had good news for us. The laws were going to be changed, allowing us to do some paid work. That was the best thing we'd heard for a long time, and we all cheered.

Then one of the supervisors came up to my room, and saw how dirty and untidy it was. He turned to me and said "It would be good if you cleaned this place up and got it more organised."

My lack of interest in life had meant I never bothered to tidy our room, and it was in a terrible mess. But now some new energy came back to me, and I got down to work. As I was cleaning the floor, I looked under my bed and saw how dusty it was. I wanted to clean there, but realised I'd have to lift the whole bed up to do it. Mine was the biggest, heaviest bed in the room, and it wouldn't be easy. However, I was feeling strong that day so I made the effort.

There was a lot of stuff under the bed but I couldn't tell what it was, for it was covered in thick dust. Amongst it all was something that looked like a book – and I was still attracted to books. So I picked it up and wiped off the dust...

It was indeed a book – but it wasn't an ordinary German book. To my amazement, it was a Persian book. On the front cover was a photo of a beautiful sunset and the words *Living Bible – New Testament*.

I hadn't read any books for a long time, but as I shook the dust off that book, something seemed to come alive in me. I wanted to start reading it at once.

First I asked around, to see if the book belonged to anyone – but no one knew anything about it. So I considered it as mine, and started to read it. I soon became intrigued by what it said, yet at the same time I was cautious. I thought, "This sounds good, but other books sound good when you sit at home reading them. The test comes when you go out and put things into practice."

I specially remember reading the sermon Jesus gave on the mountainside. One verse seemed very significant to me:

"Ask and it will be given to you; seek and you will find, knock and the door will be opened."

In a strange way I felt that the person saying these words was alive and could help me. I knew I had always been looking for something in my life. Now I began to think, maybe, just maybe, I would find what I was looking for.

I had been taught that people should first make themselves very pure, and then God might answer their prayers. Yet as I read this book, it seemed different. It seemed to say that people could find Jesus just as they are. So one night I decided to test the teaching of this book, and pray to its God. I wasn't used to praying in any Christian way, but I just asked if I would get out of that hostel and find some purpose in my life.

Five months passed, and nothing seemed to happen. Then I heard that some more Iranian refugees were coming to the hostel. I wasn't interested at first, for I felt I had nothing to say to them. I could only offer them my condolences on coming to such a horrible place. Yet when they arrived I introduced myself and asked them about themselves, as we always do.

One of them was Persian, but said he was very interested in Christianity. His name was Behnam. He had been to church in Iran and was thinking of being baptised. It was because of this that people had threatened him and he'd left Iran. I was very surprised that anyone should find Christian ideas so precious that they would leave their home country.

The other new arrival was an Armenian Iranian, from a Christian family. His name was Alex. As we talked I realised that Alex came from the same part of Tehran where I had lived. It was amazing to realise that he knew everyone I knew in that part of town, but he and I had never met before. Now, in a remote village in Germany, we were together.

I didn't tell Alex and Behnam about the New Testament I was reading. Later Alex saw it in my room and asked me about it, so I admitted I was reading it but that was all. I wanted to get to know him better, before I told him any more.

Sometimes all three of us talked together about religion, and Behnam said he believed that ultimate truth was in Jesus, and all the words of Jesus were true. Alex wasn't so sure. He said "I call myself a Christian, but I'm not a real believer in Jesus. My mother is a real believer though."

I didn't understand what he meant. Later I discovered that a real believer in Jesus is someone who invites Jesus into his heart and becomes a new person. But I didn't know that then.

Alex and Behnam brought some variety into my life, and cheered me up a bit. Sometimes Alex's mother sent parcels for him, containing various little treats and usually some Christian books as well. But Alex wasn't interested in the books. He came to me and said, "Hessam, my mother wants me to read these books and become like her. But I am young and have thousands of dreams. I don't want to become like my mother, and I don't enjoy reading. I'd be happy if you'd take all these books."

So I took every one of Alex's books, and enjoyed reading them. One was called *In God's Underground* by Richard Wurmbrant, and that book had a great influence on me. Through reading it, I understood that there are many people who are prepared to accept a lot of danger and suffering in their lives, because of their faith in Christ.

When Alex wrote to his mother, he told her I was enjoying her books. She wrote back and said, "I don't know your friend, but I believe we can all be family, whatever backgrounds we are from."

Alex knew how much his mother prayed for him, and guessed she would now include me in her prayers.

Soon after that, Alex and Behnam got transferred to a hostel in Heidelberg. They had their interviews for asylum, and both of them were accepted. I was very happy for them, but for me, life went on the same as before. My prayers didn't seem to be answered, my new friends had gone, and my spirits began to sink. My interest in Christianity got rather dampened at this time. I wasn't reading my New Testament so much, and began to think maybe I didn't deserve to have a better life.

One day Alex phoned me from Heidelberg and asked for my news. I told him how depressed I was, so he invited me to come and stay with him for a while. After getting special permission to leave the hostel, I got the train up to Heidelberg, and Alex met me at the station.

From the first moment I saw Heidelberg, I loved it. It was set among green hills and there was a big river running through the town, with a beautiful old bridge crossing it. There were interesting ships to watch, and an old castle on a hill, which was lit up at night.

The next day Alex was going to a meeting, so he asked me along too. When we got there it had already started, and I soon realised it was a Christian meeting. Alex had been too embarrassed to explain that to me before. He needn't have been, as I was very interested. I'd never been to such a meeting before.

From the start, I sensed a good atmosphere there. Some people were praying with their eyes closed, which was new to me, but I could sense their sincerity. They seemed to be worshipping God with all their hearts. The most surprising thing was that they were all Iranians and were worshipping in Persian – my mother tongue.

Then the preacher started to talk. I liked his kind and peaceful manner – it made me feel calm inside. At the end of his talk he said, "Those who are looking for a new life in Jesus Christ, who want to be a new person with Him, come forward to the front of the church."

When I heard those words, I felt as if my feet went out of my control. I couldn't sit still – I had to go forward. I said to the pastor, "I want to be a new person. I know I'm a very bad man. I can't make myself better by myself."

The pastor smiled at me and put his hand on my shoulder. "That's a very good confession," he said.

Then I found myself crying. I realised how much I was a sinner, and I asked Jesus to forgive me and to accept me as His child.

The other people in that meeting were very happy about what I'd done. They hugged me and welcomed me warmly. Alex was amazed and delighted by what had happened. He said, "I was really worried about bringing you here, but I'm so glad I did. I'm only a new Christian myself, but God has used me to help you find Jesus too."

Alex explained that soon after he'd come to Heidelberg, he'd met what he called 'real Christians' and started to go to their meetings. It hadn't been long before he had given his life to Jesus. His mother's prayers had been answered.

Over the next few days, I spent a lot of time with the Christians. Some were from Armenian families like Alex, but many were from Persian backgrounds like me. There was so much I wanted to talk to them about.

Before I left Heidelberg, my new friends all gathered round and prayed for me. One thing they prayed was that I would get a transfer to a refugee house in their city. It seemed unlikely the authorities would allow this, but we asked God for it anyway.

When I returned to my old hostel I went to the immigration office at once, to ask about a transfer. The man was very cold and unhelpful, and I was so discouraged that I phoned Alex about it. He assured me that people were still praying for me, and I shouldn't give up hope. This encouraged me, but my faith was very weak and I really didn't think this transfer was going to happen.

However, just two days later I was called back to the immigration office. I went to the same man who had seemed so stern and inflexible before – and this time his whole attitude was different. He smiled at me when I went in, and pulled a piece of paper out of a drawer in his desk. He said, "This is my agreement for your transfer to Heidelberg. You can take it and go now – but first call in at the finance department."

When I got to the finance department, they actually gave me some money for my journey. I was so excited, I hardly knew what to do. But I thanked God with all my heart.

Chapter Five

The Preacher and Writer

SO I MOVED TO HEIDELBERG, AND SOON SETTLED down. I went to all the church meetings, for I was so keen to learn. Reading the Bible became one of the most important things in my life, for I wanted to know all that God has said to mankind. It meant a lot to me that I had found the New Testament under my bed. I felt that God had spoken to me very personally and directly through that.

My life was changing drastically, and it didn't seem to be my own doing – I was sure it was God who was changing me. I wasn't instantly transformed in every area of my life, but gradually the negative things were going out of me, and more positive things were coming in. It felt like a miracle.

My desire to work for God was increasing all the time. Soon I began to preach at the Sunday meetings, and the believers encouraged me, saying I had a gift for preaching. This must have been God's work, as I was a shy person by nature, and didn't have much confidence. But God gave me confidence to speak about Him.

One of my first sermons was a message on the value of human beings. When I was younger, I used to think there wasn't much value in people, including myself. But God showed me that every single person is valuable to Him, and I wanted to share that message with everyone.

I also started writing again. It had been ages since I'd written anything creative, but when someone heard I used to write sad stories, he asked me to write a tragic story for him. So I tried, but couldn't do it. God had changed me so much, that I couldn't write sad stories any more. I remember testifying about this in church one day. I told people how I wanted to write things that would encourage people, not depress them.

Then someone suggested that we publish a monthly magazine in Persian, and I got involved in that. We called it *Rah-e-Rasti* which means 'Way of Righteousness'. I wrote my first ever Christian story for this magazine, and ended it by telling people what God had done in my own life.

All these things built up my confidence, and gradually I became a much more sociable person. I was no longer the isolated boy who avoided people and preferred the company of books. I didn't need to talk to spiders any more, for I had lots of human friends to talk to, and a wonderful Heavenly Father.

After I'd been in Heidelberg for about a year, I was given a date for an interview about my residency. So I went to my solicitor and told him I wanted to change my story. I explained that I had put my faith in Jesus Christ, and couldn't tell lies any more.

My solicitor was very interested. He pointed out that if I had become a Christian in Iran, it would have jeopardised my life and been a good reason for needing asylum. However, I told him that while I was in Iran, I hadn't been interested in Christianity at all. I realised this wouldn't help my application, but I had to tell the truth. My solicitor didn't agree with me. He told me that in my case, the truth would not work – it would only make things more complicated!

When the day of my interview came, my friends and I prayed very much, then I set off for the courtroom. When I got there I was surprised to see not one, but five people sitting in front of me, ready to question me. They asked about my new faith, and about the Bible. They asked about my activities in Heidelberg. They wanted to see my Persian Bible and one of the magazines that I helped to write.

There was a relaxed and pleasant atmosphere there in the court that day, and I felt at peace. There was one moment when I could see that my story was really gripping them. A Persian lady was translating into

German for me, and I believe it was a witness to her as well.

After one and a half hours, the court dismissed me for ten minutes. Then I was called back, and the judge announced, "We have come to the conclusion that you are a true Christian, and on behalf of the German government we are granting you residential status."

I was so excited, and so was my solicitor. He came and shook my hand and congratulated me. He said he had never seen such an interview before, and admired me for telling the truth. I gave thanks to God, and returned to Heidelberg with a heart full of joy. But that was not the end of the story. Two days later I was told my case couldn't be finalised for another month, in case there were any objections from the Central Court. I thought that was just a formality, but about a week later I was informed that the Central Court had indeed made objections. This meant I had to wait another two years and go through yet another court.

This was a terrible disappointment, and it was hard to understand why it had happened, but I trusted God would work things out for good.

The next two years actually passed very quickly, for Heidelberg is a lovely place, and I was busy at the Iranian church. When my case came to the courts again there were still some complications but finally, six years after I had arrived in Germany, I was given German travel documents, which is like a passport. I looked at it in my hand, and knew this was a gift from God. I wanted to use the new opportunities it gave me, to glorify His name.

With German residency, I could apply for higher education, and I got myself a place to study dentistry in Hamburg, northern Germany.

I was very sad to be leaving Heidelberg – it had been my spiritual birthplace and I loved it – both the city and the people. Before I left, I invited my mother to visit me there. She was so glad to see me looking happy, that she wasn't upset when I told her I was a follower of Jesus. She even commented on the peaceful atmosphere at the church where I took her.

When I got to Hamburg I was very busy with my studies, but I found time to join the Iranian church. People were very welcoming, and I realised how Christian fellowship is very special – it's a big family that extends all over the world. I don't think you can find such support and friendship amongst other people.

However, I never settled at that dentistry college. I tried hard, but felt as if the environment was killing my spirit. I thought I would be so happy there, but I wasn't at peace. I wanted to serve God, but wasn't sure what God wanted me to do. I was beginning to feel rather cut off from God, and wasn't sure why.

Then I went to an Iranian Christian conference in Denmark, and that was a real treat for me. There were Iranian believers there from all over Europe, and amongst them was a person who was to play a very special role in my life. He was the leader of an organisation called *Elam Ministries*, and he told me about an Iranian Bible college in England.

When I got back to Hamburg, I couldn't forget this Bible College. As I prayed, I felt that God was giving me permission to go and study there. So that's what I did. I felt a great peace about leaving the dentistry course, and in October 1994 I came to England and joined the Iranian Bible College. I settled down very quickly, and was sure I was in the right place.

I have now got my BA in theology from Elam College and am fully involved in writing and preaching. God has opened doors for me, that I would never have imagined.

This is still one of my favourite Bible verses, as it was so relevant to me at a crucial time in my life:

> "Ask and it will be given to you; seek and
> you will find; knock and the door will be
> opened to you."   (Matthew 7:7)

But I would like to end with this lovely
verse, for it expresses the truth about what
Jesus has done for us.

> "And He (Jesus) died for all, so that those
> who live should no longer live for
> themselves but for Him who died for them."
>   (2 Corinthians 5:15)

III

AFARIN'S STORY

"This is love: not that we loved God but
that He loved us and sent His Son..."
                              (1 John 4:10)

The Jesus Dream

The Jesus Dream

Afarin is a smallish, slim girl, with dark hair and brown eyes that usually have a lively sparkle in them. Her enthusiasm for life is refreshing and infectious, but there was a time when loneliness and disappointment nearly killed her. This is her story, in her own words.

When I was a little girl, we had a big garden, and there was a wonderful swing in it. When you were on that swing, it felt like you could fly through the air – from one side of the garden right over to the other.

Every time I went on that swing, I tried to go as high as I could. I thought that the higher I went the closer to God I would be. Even as a small child, I wanted to be near to God.

One day a strange thing happened. I was on the swing, trying to get as high as possible, when suddenly I felt I really was flying – flying in the sky. It seemed that I was up in the clouds, and God was actually there with me.

Then I heard a shout: "Afarin, what are you doing? Be careful, you'll fall."

It was my nanny calling me. Suddenly I realized where I was, and saw I'd let go of the ropes of the swing. Quickly I grabbed the ropes again – and came down off the clouds.

"What happened?" said my nanny. "Why did you let go? You must always hold on tightly, or you'll fall off and hurt yourself."

I didn't tell my nanny what had happened. I was only six years old, and hadn't the words to explain that I'd been with God, flying in the sky. I never told anyone else about it either – well, not for a long time. But I really felt I'd been with God that day, and never forgot that feeling. As long as I can remember, I so much wanted to be near Him.

The garden with the swing was in Mashhad, northern Iran. I loved it there, but soon we had to move because of my father's job. We used to move a lot, so we children had an unsettled childhood. There were five of us, three girls and two boys. We had each other to play with, but didn't get much chance to make friends outside the family, or feel we really belonged anywhere.

The worst thing about our childhood was that our mother and father didn't get on very well. They were always arguing and there was a lot of anger in our home. All of us children decided to leave home as soon as possible.

And that's what we did. When I finished school, I came to England to study. Gradually all the family came, including my parents.

But coming to England did not help my parents' marriage. In fact it got worse and finally they got divorced. It was terribly painful for me to see this happening. After that, it seemed that our family life really fell apart. We didn't get together as a family any more, except sometimes at *No Ruz* (Persian New Year). *No Ruz* is a very special time for Persian people – like Christmas is to Westerners.

Anyway, I managed to finish my studies and got a job as a computer programmer in London.

It was there that I met a boy, and fell in love. We went out together for about two years, and were engaged to be married. But in the end it didn't work out.

I felt dead inside – so hurt and disappointed. Other things were going wrong in my life too. I felt I had been let down by so many people I loved, that I didn't want to love people any more. I was very lonely, but I didn't want to share my feelings with anyone. It was partly my fear of being rejected, and partly my pride.

There was more pain to come. First I failed an important exam to do with work, but much, much worse than that – my brother was diagnosed as having leukemia. He had treatment, and we desperately hoped that a miracle would happen. But in a few months he had gone.

I was devastated. I felt that absolutely everything had gone wrong in my world.

I looked at other people's lives and it all seemed different for them. Their parents stayed together; they fell in love and married; they grew old with their brothers and sisters; they had successful lives. But for me, it didn't happen that way.

I suppose many people would have blamed God for my suffering, but I still had a deep desire to know God. I kept trying desperately hard to find him.

My parents were Muslims, so I had grown up hearing a lot about God. My parents did all the things that good Muslims should, and they frequently used the name of God when they talked. But it seemed to me that religion wasn't meaningful to my parents in a personal way – it was just part of the culture they belonged to. This wasn't enough for me – I wanted religion to mean something more real and personal. Although the religious rules seemed strict and the prayers complicated, I learnt them. I recited my prayers every day, and tried to do everything right, because I desperately wanted to please God.

Yet God was not real to me, and my prayers were never answered.

Eventually I decided that if God did exist, He must be very distant, not interested in me. Or maybe God didn't exist at all. I had done all the right things, prayed all the right prayers – but there was no sign that God was there. Then something happened that changed everything.

I was driving home from work one day when a terrible feeling of emptiness came over me. Nothing seemed worthwhile, everything seemed to have gone wrong. The God I had flown with in the sky as a child, was just a childish dream – He had never existed. If He was real he would never have let so many terrible things happen to me.

I'll never forget that time. I started to cry and I went on crying.

When I got home, I was still crying. I felt so deeply depressed and my life seemed so useless, that I wanted to kill myself. As I cried, I called out to God.

"God, if you really exist, please show yourself to me. Let something happen to show me that you are real and you hear me."

I didn't ask to actually see God. I wouldn't have dared do that, because I thought God is so powerful that if you see Him, you may die.

After I had prayed, I looked around the room and really expected something to happen. I was a bit frightened, but I hoped to see a sign of some sort. Maybe the walls would move or the flowers would change colour – something definite like that.

But nothing happened. Nothing.

I was so disappointed. I had cried to God with all my heart and believed He would answer me – but nothing had happened. I felt even more totally depressed than I'd been before.

I was also exhausted – so I lay down on my bed and fell asleep. I didn't even change my clothes ...

While I was asleep I had a dream, but it was so real it wasn't like a dream. I saw a bright light coming towards me, and as it came nearer it formed into a shape – the shape of a person. He was dressed in white, and gradually I could see his face more clearly. His face was full of love – just love.

When you see something lovely, like a new baby, you can't take your eyes off it. You want to keep looking at it, to see more and to take it all in. It was like that with me as I looked at this person's face.

I don't know why I thought He was Jesus, but I somehow just knew He was.

I said "Jesus?"

He looked at me and nodded. From the way He looked at me, I knew He really was Jesus.

His face was full of all that love; He reached out and put His hand on my shoulder. I could feel the pressure of his hand, holding my shoulder. Then He said "Don't be afraid, I am with you." *[Afarin's eyes were filling with tears as she remembered this.]*

Then He walked behind me, and the light that had been around Him faded as He went. I turned round, but He wasn't there. I wanted to follow Him, but I didn't know where He had gone.

Then I woke up, but He was still so real to me that I got out of bed and started walking round the flat looking for Him. I kept thinking, *"He is here, I saw Him, He is here somewhere."*

Suddenly I stopped, and realized it had been a dream. I'd had a dream of Jesus. I was so happy; my heart seemed to have come alive. Everything seemed completely different from before.

Soon though I started to question. "Why did I have a dream of Jesus? Why didn't I dream of one of the other prophets?"

Then I remembered I had asked God to show Himself to me. It seemed that His answer had been to show me Jesus. So I thought maybe there was a special relationship between God and Jesus, that God did not have with anyone else.

More questions came to my mind – "Could Jesus really be the Son of God, as Christian people believe?"

"No, surely not," I thought. "God is only one. He cannot have a son – can He?"

Till then I'd only thought of Jesus as a prophet, yet in my dream I had sensed He was much higher and greater than any prophet could be. I had also seen His great love in that dream – and I wanted to love Him too. Something about Him had touched my heart very deeply.

I wanted to know more about Him, to talk to people about Him, but I didn't know what to do. I didn't have a Bible I could read, or any Christian friends to talk to. However, every time I thought about my dream I felt a great joy inside me. This joy lifted me and made me want to keep praising God. It gave me new hope for the future.

After a while, I told my mother about my dream. Her reaction was interesting. She said, "That's good. Jesus is one of our prophets. It's good to dream of Him."

That wasn't enough for me. I wanted to hear more about Jesus – but what could I do? I couldn't share these things with everyone. So I kept it hidden in my heart. I could never forget it.

About six months passed, then something amazing happened. I think I met an angel. Let me explain.

I was away on a computer programming course and one day I went to the canteen, looking for somewhere to eat my sandwiches. The place was full, but then I saw a table occupied by just one young man. He was dark haired and a bit middle-Eastern looking. I asked him if I could sit there, and he said, "Yes, of course."

So I sat down and began to eat my sandwiches. The young man was reading a book, and I noticed there was a picture of an Eastern-looking woman on the back cover. That really interested me. When I managed to see the title, I became even more curious. It was called – *I Dared To Call Him Father*.‡

I knew that Christians called God 'Father', and some of them also called their pastors 'Father'. So I guessed this was a Christian book. I was so interested that I plucked up courage and said, "Excuse me, what is that book about?"

"It is about a Pakistani lady who comes to know Jesus Christ, and it changes her life," he replied.

‡   *I Dared To Call Him Father* is the autobiography of Bilquis Sheikh, a wealthy Pakistani lady. She has some unusual dreams, finds herself drawn to read the Bible, and comes to a deep faith in Jesus Christ.

Suddenly my dream of Jesus came in front of my eyes like a film, and I felt my heart beating very loudly. I wanted to grab the young man's book and start reading it. Instead I asked him, "How did she come to know Jesus Christ?"

"You will have to read the book," he said.

"Please could I borrow it – after you have finished with it? I am here for just one week on a course, but I promise I will give it back."

"Yes that's OK. I am reading the last pages, then you can have it."

After a few minutes, he gave me the book. I asked him where I could find him to give it back, and he said, "I work here. You can always find me here."

I said "Here in this canteen?"

He said "Yes."

I was so excited to get this book, that as soon as I got back to my room, I started to read it. The more I read, the more gripped I was. Some of the dreams this Pakistani lady had were similar to mine. It brought me to tears. I felt my love for Jesus was growing, and I longed even more to know Him better.

I went back several times to that canteen, to return the book, but I never saw the young man again. I looked everywhere in the college, but I couldn't find him.

Now as I look back, I think he may have been an angel from God. Of course I can't be sure about that, but it was strange that he said he would always be there, but I never saw him again.

Now I felt I belonged to Jesus in some way, and I longed for someone to help me get to know Him better. But I didn't know who to ask. I was afraid of being laughed at or rejected. So I asked God Himself to help me – there didn't seem to be anyone else.

However, several months went by and nothing happened. So I decided I would do something about it – I would go to a church. I went out one Sunday morning, and walked around looking for one. I saw a woman and asked her: "Do you know the way to a church?"

She said "What sort of church?"

I said "A church of Jesus Christ".

She pointed me to a church and I went in, and sat down. I watched the others there, and tried to do what they did. When they stood up, I stood up. When they sat down, I sat down. When the service finished, they all went out. Nobody greeted me, nobody wanted to know who I was or why I'd come. They said quick hellos to each other, and that was it. Nothing else.

I stayed there for a while, sitting there and looking at the books they had given me – a Bible and a hymnbook. I wanted to take the Bible home with me, but I was too scared. I thought maybe I could ask the pastor if he could let me have a Bible, but then a man came up to me and said:

"Excuse me, lady, the service is finished."

I wanted to ask if he could help me, but I hadn't liked the way he'd spoken. Something shut my mouth and I couldn't say anything at all. I just left the books, and went out. I said to myself, "If that is the church, I don't want to go there again. I will forget about churches."

About two months later my mother was round at my flat, and she told me she'd met a young Iranian couple who were Christians. I immediately thought she meant they were Armenian Iranians (who are practically always Christian, at least in name). She said "No, they are Persian Iranians, and they are Christians."

"How is that possible?" I said. "Persian Iranians cannot be Christians."

"But they are," she replied. "And they go to an Iranian church."

"It must be an Armenian Church," I said.

"No, it really is an Iranian church, and it's quite near here."

"I've never seen any Iranian church, and I've been living here a whole year."

"Well there is one, and these people are going to take me there."

I could hardly believe it, but it turned out that my mother had met this couple in the market some time before. She had already been to their house, and to some of their church home-group meetings. She had met a lot of Christians but had said nothing about it to me – nothing at all.

I was really excited to hear about this church, and these people. My mother was going with the young couple to the next church service, so I asked her to invite them back to my flat for dinner afterwards.

When the next Sunday came, my mother went to church, and I stayed home and cooked dinner. It was about 2 o'clock when they all arrived back at my place. As soon as I saw the Christian couple, I liked them. They had such kind faces.

After dinner they started telling me about Jesus, but I stopped them and told them about my dream. I was bubbling with excitement, for I'd been longing to tell some Christians about it for a long time. It was wonderful to actually have Iranian Christians to share it with.

When they heard all that had happened, they were amazed. They'd thought they were coming to talk to me about Jesus, but I was telling them about my own experience of Him.

I told them I was looking for a Bible, and they handed me their own. I took it and looked at it in awe. It was the first time I had held a Persian Bible in my hand. It was in my own mother tongue and it felt such a very precious thing.

After they had gone, I started to read that Bible. I read and read the gospels, because they are about Jesus. I was so hungry to know more about Jesus, the person who had comforted me when I needed help so badly.

As I read, I saw that God is a God of love. I also realized there can be a very special relationship between God and a believer. It can be a relationship of love and fellowship, of knowing each other personally.

The next Sunday I went to the Iranian church for the first time. I specially liked it because I could see the people loved Jesus like I did. I felt a bit shy, but people were very kind. Some were really excited to meet me. They had never met me before, but said they'd been praying for me, because my mother had told them about me.

At one point they sang a song in Persian, which touched me deeply. As I listened, it brought me to tears. I cried and cried, but it was with joy, for the song spoke of the things that were in my heart. It goes like this:

Come to me Jesus, and be my guide,
I am putting myself into Your hands,

You are my good guide and my friend,
My soul thirsts for You, for Your presence.

My request is that You always be my guide,
I will not open my heart and let anyone else in.
I want only Your presence, my crucified Jesus,
I trust in You – always be my guide.

Rule in my heart,
You are my beloved Jesus.

I cried because those words said just what I wanted to say.

After that, I went to every church meeting that there was. I was thrilled to be in the place that God had led me to, and wanted to learn all I could about Jesus. When I had my dream I knew very little about Jesus. I just knew Him as a person who was full of love and who loved me. Now I learnt that He is my Saviour. All my sin has been forgiven because Jesus died for me on the cross. I asked Him to take over my life in every way, and prayed I would become the person He wanted me to be.

Gradually my attitude towards life and people began to change. I started loving people and enjoying being with them. I stopped worrying so much, for I was learning to trust God more. There was much more peace inside me, and the emptiness I used to feel was going away.

I also learnt that as well as being my Saviour, Jesus is my friend. He is the one true friend who will never leave me. I wanted to follow Him in every way, and one way was being baptised. However I still had some fears and doubts – till one day when I told one of the church elders about my dream. He listened to me, then opened his Bible and showed me Isaiah 43:5. It says "Do not be afraid, for I am with you".

It was wonderful for me to see those words written there, for they were the words I had heard in my dream. Before then, I hadn't realised those words came from the Bible.

As time passed, I became more active in church life. Now I help to encourage new believers, and am involved in doing the catering for special events. I have found a lot of new friends – good friends. My friends are very close to me, and I feel part of a big family in the church.

One day I heard about a Christian conference called *Spring Harvest.* Ten thousand Christians would gather there to worship God. I so much wanted to be there, but they told me it was too late. All the places were booked.

I kept saying to God "I want to go to *Spring Harvest,* I want to go to *Spring Harvest*".

Then one day I was driving my car when suddenly I heard a voice from the back of the car saying, "Afarin, go. Just drive and go there."

I knew that voice – it was the same voice I'd heard in my dream. I felt such a joy in my heart – I wanted to jump up and down. But before I could go, I had to ask my boss for a week off work. I was asking with just one day's notice, so I was nervous about it. But when he heard where I was going, he gave me the time off. That also seemed like a mini-miracle, and I was even more sure that God wanted me to go.

So I packed and drove to Skegness the next day. They had told me the conference was fully booked, but I was amazed at what God provided for me. At the last minute a family had cancelled their booking for a caravan, so I could stay there. It was a beautiful caravan – everything in it was new.

It was really wonderful to be there at *Spring Harvest,* seeing thousands of people of different backgrounds worshipping God together.

After that, my faith became even stronger. I still have problems sometimes, and my life has its ups and downs. But the Holy Spirit has come into my life, and God's love goes on getting deeper and deeper into my heart.

———————

It was the thought of thousands of people meeting together to worship God, that had made Afarin so keen to go to *Spring Harvest.*

For she has a passion for worship. Her experience of God's love has given her a tremendous love for Him and a longing to express this in worship. She also has a great heart for people, and is sensitive to their needs. People feel lifted closer to God as she pours out her heart in prayer for them. They sense His love touching them through her love and prayers.

When she was a small child Afarin had swung high on a swing, trying to get close to God. One day she had felt she was really up in the clouds – 'flying with God'. Then things went wrong, and it seemed that 'flying with God' was an impossible dream.

But when she came to know Jesus, it changed everything. She began again, in a very real way, to fly with God – and to carry others along with her.

THIS IS MY TRUE STORY

I thank You Lord, for my true story
Rejoice for what You have done for me.
It's hard to put my feeling into words.
It seems like a play in a scene or a dream.
But only You know, this is my true story.

You created me to be your sweet child.
You loved me even before I was born.
You held my hand when I was on my swing.
You played with me when I was flying in the sky.
But only You know, this is my true story.

I've grown up without knowing Your love for me.
I blamed You for all my failure in my life.
I suffered so much for not knowing You my Lord.
I sinned, I sinned only to You my God, please forgive me.
But only You know, this is my true story.

You heard me when I cried out to You.
You helped me when I was dying to know You.
You embraced me in my dream with Your loving smile.
You told me, "Don't be afraid! I am with you".
But only You know, this is my true story.

I cried with joy for what I heard from You.
I trust You! Always be my guide my Lord.
I want only Your presence, my crucified, my hope.
I love You with all my heart, You are my beloved Jesus.
But only You know, this is my true story.

Afarin,   Jan 2000

IV

DR HEDAYAT'S STORY

"Blessed is the man.... He is like a tree
planted by streams of water, which yields
its fruit in season and whose leaf does not
wither..."   (from Psalm One)

The Tree that Bears Fruit

The Tree that bears Fruit

DR HEDAYAT IS IN HIS LATE SIXTIES NOW, BUT
has a tough, wiry look about him and is very
sprightly in body, mind and spirit. He has
thick greyish white hair and an expressive
face that is usually creased up in a wide
disarming smile.

However, in his earlier life he did not smile
so often. Although he was well respected as a
doctor in the Iranian town of Ghazvin, he was
also considered to be a bad-tempered man,
prone to dark moods. To some people, his only
love seemed to be money – certainly not God.

Yet Dr Hedayat's mother, Miriam, had
always believed her son would be a godly
man, because before he was born she had a
strange and vivid dream. He explains:

Before I was born – before I was even con-
ceived, my mother had this dream. She saw a
man with white robes, white hair and a white
beard. This man came to her and said, 'You are
going to have a son – call him Hedayat.'

When she woke up, she told my father about
the dream and asked him, 'Who is this man?
Our prophets have black hair and beards, not
white.'

My father didn't know who the man could be, so my mother asked other people. Some said, 'This sounds like the prophet Elijah. Maybe this dream is of him. He is not a prophet of your own religion.'

Later my mother realised she was pregnant, and after I was born she asked my father 'What am I going to call him?'

He said 'Give him the name you were told in your dream.'

So I was called Hedayat.

Chapter One

The Book Lover

HEDAYAT'S PARENTS LIVED IN SHIRAZ – THE "city of roses and poets", on a high plain in the south of Iran. Its most famous and best-loved poets are Hafez and Saadi, who lived in Shiraz in the 13th and 14th centuries. Both Hafez and Saadi wrote about Jesus with great respect. Hafez also mentions the Jewish prophet Elijah in some of his poems.‡

So baby Hedayat was born into a city that honoured its poets, and its poets honoured Jesus. This had a deep effect on Hedayat's family, especially his mother Miriam. She spent a lot of time reading the old Persian poetry.

Hedayat was Miriam's only child, and they became very close. When he was sick, she usually took him to the Christian hospital in Shiraz, and it was there that he got his first impressions of Jesus. They used to show filmstrips there, which told stories from the Bible. One thing that stayed vividly

---

‡   One of Hafez's poems says "may Elijah come back to us, then our sadness will leave us". Elijah is known as Elias in Islam.

in his mind was a picture of Jesus with a crown of thorns on His head, and a little lamb in his arms

When Hedayat grew up, he decided he wanted to be a doctor, so he left Shiraz to go to a medical school in another area of Iran. That medical school was renowned for its open-minded atmosphere, where students spent a lot of time discussing different philosophies of life. This suited young Hedayat, who was a great thinker and loved to explore new ideas.

Some of his fellow students were communists, who were very active in Iran at that time. Hedayat respected their enthusiasm and read several of their books, including Marx's *Das Kapital*. He noticed that it called itself the gospel for working people and this interested him, as he had thought the gospel was just a Christian book. He wondered what the word 'gospel' really meant, and what the difference was between the Christians' gospel and the communists' gospel.

After reading a lot of the communist literature, Hedayat decided it was not for him. He was still interested in the 'gospel' though, and when a neighbour invited him along to a church he agreed to go. A man called Mahmud Jalili was speaking in the church that day. Hedayat forgot most of what he said, but he remembered these words: *All people need to be saved, and Jesus Christ is the Saviour of the world.*

Rev. Jalili explained that people need to be saved because of their sin. When Hedayat heard this he said to himself, "I don't need to be saved – I haven't done anything wrong. Compared to a lot of people, I'm a very good man."

He had not understood Rev. Jalili's message, but it had touched him and he wanted to hear more about Jesus. He liked Rev. Jalili, who had a very sweet spirit as well as a strong faith. So he went back to the church again – and again. He also met an American missionary there[‡] and began to go to his Bible classes.

Throughout this time, Hedayat was working hard at his medical studies, and soon he qualified as a doctor. Now he was "Dr Hedayat" – a title that brought great respect from the community. He was still interested in studying the Bible and went to the church regularly, so eventually the church leaders asked the young doctor if he wanted to be baptised. He said he did – but in his heart he didn't feel ready for it. He only agreed out of respect for his Bible teacher, and when the time came for the baptism service, he didn't turn up.

[‡]   This was William Miller, a famous Presbyterian missionary to Iran. He has written Mahmud Jalili's story in a book called *Ten Muslims meet Christ*.

However, Dr Hedayat's Christian friends believed the young doctor really did have a love for Jesus, so a few months later they asked him about baptism again. Again he said he wanted it, and this time he <u>did</u> turn up on the day.

Dr Hedayat's friends were right about him having a love for Jesus. But although he'd learnt a lot from the Bible, he still hadn't understood about Jesus being His Saviour. He didn't think he needed a Saviour, because he couldn't see any sin in his life. Looking back, he explains it this way:

> I hadn't really recognised my sin and repented of it. I thought Jesus Christ was just a man – a good moral teacher who lived long ago. He was not alive in me as a person, as He is now. That's something else. Hallelujah!

It was to be many more years before Dr Hedayat could say Jesus was alive in him as a person. After his baptism he continued to be involved in church activities for a while, but then he lost interest and gradually drifted away. He was still open to different ideas, so he tried reading books about his parent's religion. But they didn't draw him to that faith at all – in fact they had the opposite effect. So he decided to forget about God and concentrate his energies on the things of this world – making money and establishing a family.

After specialising in radiology, Dr Hedayat moved to a town called Ghazvin – a town close to some mountains and a beautiful lake. He set up his own private X-ray clinic and also got a job in a local hospital. Having got himself settled, he married a girl from a neighbouring town. Later he invited his mother to come and live with them, as his father had died some years earlier.

It wasn't long before the children arrived. First they had a little boy, whom they called Manouchehr. Two years later a little girl, Shekufeh, came along. The next year another little girl arrived, Afsaneh. Soon the courtyard of their house was full of toys and children's bicycles.

Dr Hedayat had a very keen, active mind, and wanted to know everything about everything. As his children grew up he wanted them to follow his example, and they have many memories of the ways he got them to learn things. Manouchehr recalls:

Our Dad read a lot of books in both English and Persian, and he encouraged us children to read them too. He also played us a lot of records of classical music. His favourite was Tchaikovsky's "Swan Lake". We all knew it by heart after a while.

There was a big lake quite near us, and Dad would often take us for picnics there, or into the mountains. He loved walking in the mountains, and was also very interested in astronomy. He spent a lot of time studying the stars.

Sometimes he would take us all out at night, into the mountains where the air was very clean. We would look up into the sky, and he would get us searching for certain stars. He would know their names, what they were like and how far away they were.

These things were fun – but my father was not always an easy man to relate to in those early days.

When Manouchehr said that his father was not always an easy man to relate to, he was making an understatement. For although the doctor was proud of his family, he was often impatient with them, and they were aware that he had a dark side. On the surface, he may have looked like a very successful man – but in his heart there was a growing emptiness.

By now, Dr Hedayat had cut off all connections with Christians. Occasionally some poignant memories came back to him, of those people and their Jesus – but most of the time he pushed them out of his mind. What filled his mind now was making money – as much as possible.

He had already become very wealthy, but the more he had, the more he wanted. He would lend money to people but demand a lot of interest, and become threatening if they could not pay him back. He became the sort of person whom people tried to avoid. Some would cross the road if they saw him coming along the street.

Although he would say he didn't care what people thought of him, he didn't like what he had become. As time passed by, he began to wonder whether some evil powers were at work in his life. Whenever his mind wasn't occupied in work or reading books, he was aware of evil inside him and around him. He kept having foul, twisted thoughts. They weren't just temptations to do wrong – they were terrible thoughts of death and decay and Hell.

In the summer of 1970, things came to a head as he explains.

One night I felt so bad. There seemed to be nothing but rottenness inside me, and I felt as if a great darkness was overwhelming me.

Then I remembered what Rev. Mahmud Jalili had said many years earlier. **'All people are sinners and need to be saved. Jesus Christ is the Saviour of the world.'**

As I thought about this, I asked myself 'Where is this Jesus now? They say He is in heaven, but I can't go there.'

Then I lifted my heart to heaven and cried out in desperation – 'O Jesus, I know I am a very bad person, and I need help. If you are really alive and can change people, can you do something for me?'

When I went to sleep that night, I hoped to have a dream or vision of Jesus – but it didn't happen. I woke up the next morning to find everything the same as before. So I went off to work at the hospital as usual.

At about ten o'clock, I came out of my office. I had just started to walk across the hospital yard, when I saw three men coming towards me. I knew one of them, for he worked at the hospital, but I didn't know the other two. One looked like an Iranian, the other one looked like a foreigner.

A few days before Dr Hedayat had cried out to Jesus, a small team of booksellers had driven out of Tehran. It was summer time and very hot, so they planned to spend a few days visiting the cooler areas of Iran. They found somewhere to camp, then went out from there to sell books in nearby towns.[‡]

On the last day of their trip, two of them were dropped off in the town of Ghazvin. They usually went to shops and offices to sell their books, but on that occasion they found themselves looking at a hospital. They hesitated, wondering what sort of welcome they might get, then decided to go in.

‡   They were an international team consisting of two Iranians, two Englishmen, and one American. They belonged to "Operation Mobilisation" – an organisation which encourages people to distribute Christian books and talk to people about Jesus.

Once inside, they met a man at the reception who was friendly and helpful. When they explained why they were there, he said he would take them to a doctor – a doctor who read a lot of books.

The three men set off across the yard towards the doctor's office...

Dr Hedayat looked at the men coming towards him, with great interest. He wanted to know who they were and what they were doing, for foreigners didn't often visit Ghazvin. The man from the hospital greeted him and explained, "These two men are booksellers. I was bringing them to you, for I know you love books."

The doctor was intrigued and asked, "What kind of books do you have?"

"Look and see," they replied, opening their cases.

As soon as he saw the books, Dr Hedayat realised they were Christian ones. He was amazed, and a wonderful feeling of hope came over him. He thought, "Just last night I called to Jesus and He has answered at once, by sending these men to me."

The doctor didn't tell the men what he was thinking, but he felt very excited as he looked through their books, deciding which to buy. He ended up buying a lot.

As soon as he got home that evening, he chose one of the books and sat down to read it. It was *World Aflame* by Billy Graham, and soon he was engrossed. This book gives an overall summary of the main themes of the Bible, and as Dr Hedayat turned the pages, more and more things fell into place in his mind. He began to understand the Bible message that when Jesus Christ was killed, He was accepting the punishment that human beings deserve, for all the things they do wrong. That was why Jesus was called the Saviour of the world, who saves people from their sins.

Many years earlier, Dr Hedayat had heard those same words but they hadn't made sense to him. In those days he hadn't thought he had any sins, so he didn't think he needed a saviour. Now he was older, it was different. He sensed that evil was gnawing away at his whole being. The word 'gospel', that had puzzled him in his student days, now made sense. He realised it meant 'good news' – and the Christian gospel was the good news about Jesus Christ. It was completely different from the communists' good news.

At the end of *World Aflame*, the author asks "Are you ready to give your life to Jesus?" As Dr Hedayat read those words, he felt the presence of God come over him. It didn't seem like a book speaking to him – it seemed like God, speaking to his heart. And God was asking him to give his life to Jesus. He knew this could be the biggest decision

he would ever make in his life – and he
didn't want to rush into it.

First I thought it over – I was balancing it up. I
wanted to accept Jesus as Saviour – but there
was a struggle going on inside me.

Then I said to myself 'Yes, I'm ready. I really
do want to give my life to Jesus.'

When I said that, it seemed as if I had touched
Jesus and He had touched me. I felt someone
coming into me, bringing a power – a power of
peace and goodness.

I also felt as if something was going out of me.
I really believe it was demons and all their evil
going out, and the Lord Jesus coming in with
His love.

Then I stood up and was sure I'd had a new
birth – a spiritual new birth. On that day I
became a new man.

The booksellers got back to their camp that
night, thinking it had been an ordinary day,
much like any other. They did not know how
strong a seed of faith had been sown in a
man's heart that day. Nor had they any idea
what would happen to that seed in years to
come.

To the onlooker, it might have seemed
unlikely that Dr Hedayat's faith would
survive very long. There were no Christians
in his family, and no church in his town.
Also, the Iranian revolution was only a few
years away, when opposition to anyone who

was not a Muslim would get much fiercer –
especially in small towns like Ghazvin.

**A seed had been sown – but into very
hard ground...**

Chapter Two

Birth of a family church

IN THE DAYS OF HAFEZ AND SAADI (the Old Persian poets), there were far more Persian Christians in Iran than there are today. They were part of the Eastern Nestorian church, that was flourishing all over Central Asia at that time. Iran also had larger populations of Jews and Zoroastrians in those days. They, like the Christians, had been in Iran since pre-Islamic days and all these different communities were well accepted in Persian society.

However, today many Iranians think "to be Persian is to be Muslim". Such people often feel that any Persian who chooses to follow another faith, is a traitor to their country as well as to Islam.‡ If the "traitor" is someone in their own family, they would feel it as a terrible disgrace, and consider it their duty to disown them. They might even kill the "traitor" – or others in their community might do so.

When Dr Hedayat decided to give his life to Jesus, he was very aware of the

‡   In some countries, leaving Islam is a crime that carries the death penalty.

problems he might face, especially with his own family. But the change in his character was so dramatic, it seemed like a miracle to the people around him. He really did seem like a "new man" and they couldn't help but be impressed. His wife Faribah was the first to notice the difference. She said, "What's happened to you, you're so different – so happy." He replied, "I asked Jesus into my life, and He has changed me."

His children never forgot that time. One day their father had been easily irritated with them – the next day he was very kind and patient. They waited a few days to see if it would last, then went to him and said "Daddy, you're always cheerful and loving now. We like it."

The family's daily routine soon changed drastically. For many years, Dr Hedayat had got up at five in the morning. He would read the paper and smoke a cigarette, before going walking in the mountains with some neighbours. But now he started getting up even earlier, to read the Bible and pray. He would still go off to the mountains, but would sing enthusiastic songs of praise to God as he walked. He would talk freely to his companions about Jesus – he wasn't at all shy or embarrassed about his new faith. After getting home, he would gather his wife and children around him and they would all read the Bible and pray together – before having breakfast.‡

For more teaching and fellowship, Dr Hedayat also started going to a church in Tehran. It was a long bus journey away, but he went regularly and sometimes took his children with him.

After a couple of years, he decided to tell his story publicly in church. When he got to the part where two men came to his hospital selling books, a young Englishman in the congregation got increasingly excited. He realised that he knew these two booksellers – he had been part of their team that summer. He hadn't actually been to the hospital with them, but it was a tremendous encouragement for him to hear how God had worked through his team-mates. It was also an encouragement to Dr Hedayat when he talked to the Englishman later, and realised what an appropriate day he had chosen to tell his story. It was one of the very few times that the young bookseller had ever been to that church – he usually worshipped at another.

Dr Hedayat was very keen that all his family should get as much Bible teaching as possible, and his wife and children didn't object to this. They were happy to be

‡   Dr Hedayat also went to go to bed very early. Manouchehr remembers how he couldn't speak to his Dad after 9pm – he was so sleepy.

learning about something that had changed a bad-tempered, irritable man to someone full of fun and laughter. It was different though, for the doctor's mother Miriam. When he told her he had become a Christian, she was devastated and didn't want to believe it. When he assured her it was true, she said "Son, I don't want to live with you any more".

This reaction was not surprising, for in Iran, to change your religion is to reject your family.

Miriam still owned a house in Shiraz, so she went to live there. Dr Hedayat grieved, for he was afraid he might never see her again. But a few months later, her story took an unexpected turn, as she came back to Ghazvin saying "My son, I'm very ill." She pointed to a place on her neck and said "If I try and eat something, it sticks here in my throat."

Dr Hedayat took her for a special barium X-ray at once, but when he looked at the pictures, his heart sank. He got some further tests done, but they only confirmed the terrible news – she had cancer of the oesophagus. This sort of cancer is almost impossible to treat successfully, and the doctor knew it. Without going into all the details, he told his mother she couldn't go back to Shiraz to live by herself. He asked her to stay with them in Ghazvin – and she agreed.

As he thought of what his mother was facing, Dr Hedayat felt very depressed. So he prayed, and looked for books about the healing power of Jesus. One was called *I Believe in Miracles* by Katherine Kuhlman. As he read that book, he kept wishing he could take his mother to Katherine Kuhlman. Then he sensed God's voice saying, "*You* pray, my son. *You* pray. Katherine Kuhlman is not the one who heals – *I am.*" Dr Hedayat took those words to heart:

My mother was in Tehran for tests, and they decided to give her cobalt treatment. Just before they started it, they gave me a small sample of her tumour in a jar. They told me to take it to a laboratory the next morning. So for one night I had that jar, and I stood it on a shelf in the house.

The next morning I got up at 4 a.m. as usual, for my time of prayer. As I prayed, I looked up at the jar on the shelf and in my mind I could see an evil spirit in that tumour. I stood up and looked at the tumour and said, 'I kill you. Die – you evil spirit.'

I watched the tumour carefully, and it did not change physically. But in my mind I could see it shrink and become very small, like a dried up bit of dead meat. Then something in my heart said, *'She is healed – she is healed.'*[‡]

My heart was full of joy, and I said 'Thank you, Jesus. You healed my mother.'

As soon as I saw my mother again, I said to her 'Mother you're healed.' She stared at me – and so did the other people there. Some of them laughed, and I could see they thought I was out of my mind. My mother just said quietly 'Yes my son.'

She didn't believe me; she only said it to please me. But after the cobalt treatment she had more tests done, and they were completely free of any sign of cancer.

At first Miriam couldn't believe she was healed. It was still hard for her to swallow solid things, and her family had to coax her to eat little bits of bread again. Gradually she got back to eating normally and regained her strength, but she never accepted that God had healed her through prayer. She even began to say she'd never had cancer, even though the X-rays and biopsy results had made it very clear.

Dr Hedayat went on praying for his mother. He kept hoping that one day she would tell him she'd accepted Jesus as her

[‡]   Dr Hedayat knows that illnesses can be caused by bacteria and viruses, and agrees with scientific ways of treating them. But he also believes that evil spirits can cause illnesses.

Saviour – but she never did. However, she continued living with her son and his family, and became very accepting of the many Christians that came to visit them. She would often stay in the room when they were praising God together.

Towards the end of her life, Miriam would repeatedly read the poems of Hafez that mentioned Jesus. She said they made her feel at peace. For this and other reasons, her son was sure she had a love for Jesus in her heart. Maybe her response to Him had all started when she accepted the word of a man in a dream – a man with white robes and white hair. People had told her this man was not of her own religion – yet she and her husband had acted on his instructions when they called their baby Hedayat.

Miriam only told her son about that dream towards the end of her life. She thought the white-haired man was probably the Jewish prophet Elijah, but Dr Hedayat's mind instantly went to the verses in Revelation, where the Apostle John has a vision of Jesus dressed in white, with white hair.

Miriam lived for eight years after her healing from cancer, and in the end it was not cancer that she died of. Just before she died, she said to her son:

Son, you tell me you have visions. Now I too have had a vision, but I don't know what it means. In my vision, you and I and some other relatives were all together in a very beautiful place. But I don't know where it was.

The relatives Miriam saw in her vision were some who had shown great respect for Dr Hedayat's faith. When talking with him, they referred to Jesus as 'the one whose name is always in your mouth' – and this was said in a kindly way. They never criticised him for his faith in Jesus – sometimes they told him wistfully that they wished they were more like him. They often asked him to pray for them.

When his mother died, Dr Hedayat mourned deeply for her. Yet he had a sense of peace about it. He believed she had had a vision of heaven, and felt that God was telling him, "She is with me now." As he thought about his mother and her relatives, Dr Hedayat said:

> We cannot tell what is going on in people's hearts. Salvation is always through Jesus, but there are many different ways of coming to God through Him. There are also many unexpected places we can find Him.

> All of creation points to Jesus Christ. When we look at the world around us, at the things He has made, we can see Him. When I look at everything, I see Jesus.

It had taken a long time for Miriam to accept her son's new faith, but this wasn't the case for Faribah, his wife. She was delighted by the dramatic change in her husband and when he told her it was because of Jesus, she wanted to know this Jesus for herself.

However, her biggest problem was understanding why Jesus had died. When she tried reading the Bible, she found it very hard going. Dr Hedayat spent a lot of time explaining the gospel to her, but she couldn't understand it. As time passed, she saw her children experience God's presence in dramatic ways, and she desperately wanted to have a similar experience herself. But it didn't happen that way, and she found this very disappointing. Sometimes she would say, "I don't think Jesus wants me."

Her family were very upset when she talked like that. However, she continued to join them for their Bible readings and prayers and sometimes went to church with them. When their Christian friends came to the house, she would happily serve them tea and meals.

Dr Hedayat valued his wife highly. He says "I'm sure God chose her for me. She was a great support to me over the years – a very good companion and helper." The children adored their mother. Manouchehr noticed how she never argued with his father, and never said anything negative about her family's faith in Jesus.

Faribah's faith seemed to grow with time, but it had a lot of ups and downs. She was reluctant to call herself a Christian – especially publicly. Then, much later in her life, her faith became firmer. She began to openly call herself a believer in Jesus Christ – even in front of her brother and other relatives. That was a big thing for her. ‡

However, the end of Faribah's life was a very hard time for her and all the family. Although many people were praying for her, she was ill for a long time and did not recover. It was hard for her children to understand why their mother was not healed. She was still relatively young, and their grandmother had experienced a miraculous healing at a much greater age.

No one can answer these questions. But something very precious happened, just as Faribah was dying. This is how Dr Hedayat describes it:

> In the last weeks of my wife's life, the children and I spent a lot of time by their mother's bed, praying for her. Manouchehr was a very keen Christian by that time, and when it seemed his mother was about to go to God, he asked 'Mother, do you want to share the bread and wine of our Lord?'

> His mother said 'Yes, I am ready.'

‡ Her problem was understandable, for the word "Christian" has negative associations for many Muslims – who have not forgotten the atrocities of the Crusades. Some think that all Western society is "Christian" and are appalled by its lack of morality. For these reasons, many who come to faith in Jesus prefer simply to call themselves "believers" or "followers of Jesus".

She took the bread and wine, then as we sat on her bed praying, she died. I knew she had died. There was no heartbeat, no respiration. I was at the foot of the bed, my son Manouchehr was at her head, and our daughters Shekufeh and Afsaneh were there too.

Yes, she died, but in that moment her face was changed. Her skin changed, and her face became alive like a newborn baby. All of us could see it. We were there, all four of us, and we all saw it. Manouchehr remembers this very well, and so do his sisters. Each one could see this wonderful testimony, of how their mother's face changed.

I believe she was seeing the Lord. We all felt that wonderful presence of God, strongly there with us. Then again as we watched her, we saw a change in her face again. There was a little movement of life on her skin. Then her hand moved up to her heart, and her spirit left her.

If you had been there you would have seen it too – the wonderful changes in her face and the way her spirit left her. We all saw it; and we were so glad, we were full of joy.

I told the children, 'God breathed the breath of life into the first man's nose, and when a person is dying it comes out again.'

This was a very hard time for us, but we must remember that everything that happens to us has been allowed by God. We cannot always understand Him, but we have to trust Him. His ways are far greater than ours.

Some things may look good to us and some may look bad, but God does not look at things like a man does. We must trust God about everything, even when we don't understand what He is doing. The Bible says 'in all things God works for the good of those who love him.' (Romans 8:28).

From the first day of his spiritual 'new birth', Dr Hedayat had tried to help all his household come to know Jesus. It had been a struggle for both the older ladies, and neither of them talked very much about their faith. But it was different for the children. Once they came to know Jesus, they couldn't stop talking about it – and it was through them that a new church came into being.

This didn't happen all at once. Manouchehr, Shekufeh and Afsaneh loved their father's new faith from the beginning, but it took time for it to make sense to them. Manouchehr explains:

I remember when my father started telling us things about Jesus. We were very interested, but didn't understand much of what he said. Every now and again he would ask me if I had assurance that my sins had been forgiven. I didn't like to disappoint him, but I always had to say 'no'.

This went on for about a year. Dad would sometimes take us to Tehran to church with him, but we were very young and it was hard for us to understand the teaching. Then one day when I was about eleven years old, someone at church was preaching about the Cross – and God touched my heart through that. I suddenly understood what Jesus had done for me – and I gave myself to Him.

When I did that, I felt I'd been 'born again'. Things started to fall into place for me, and our family prayers and Bible reading made more sense. You can imagine how pleased my father was.

About a year after Manouchehr had that experience, he and his sisters went to a Christian children's camp in Tehran. It was led by Rev. Sam Yeghnazar, who is now pastor of the Iranian church in London. As the days passed by, many of the children asked Jesus to be their Saviour.

On the last day of the camp, something very wonderful happened. About sixty children were in a big tent, praying together and crying out to the Lord for His blessing. As they prayed, the Spirit of God fell and they were all filled with the Holy Spirit. In response their hearts overflowed with worship and praise. They felt that heaven had come down to earth.

All three of Dr Hedayat's children were at that meeting. Up till then, Afsaneh and Shekufeh, hadn't known anything like the 'new birth' that their brother Manouchehr had experienced. But now they had – though they were only nine and ten years old. Manouchehr remembers:

It was an amazing time for everyone. Once I'd started praying I could hardly stop myself. I went on for about an hour, and so did many others. It was really VERY special. That sort of thing didn't happen often.

When the children got back to Ghazvin, they kept hold of their new closeness to God. They were so enthusiastic about their faith that they started to invite school friends to their house for worship meetings. Then those friends invited brothers and sisters and other friends. Dr Hedayat would welcome them all, and talk to them about Jesus.

The seed had put down roots, and was shooting up into a vigorous plant.

By this time (the summer of 1972), most people in Ghazvin knew about Dr Hedayat's faith. When he started telling people he was a Christian, it had been the talk of the town. This is how one local puts it:

Dr Hedayat was a well-known character in the town, and when he changed so suddenly and dramatically, everyone was talking about it. They were astonished at what had happened. The bad-tempered money-grabber had become cheerful and generous. Instead of demanding that people repay their debts, he was very easy-going about it. He would forgive the debt entirely, or would say 'If you can't pay me back yet – don't worry. Wait till it's easy for you.' If anyone commented on his change of attitude, he would tell them that Jesus Christ had changed him.

This was all so amazing, that when people heard they could come to the doctor's house to find out more – they came. Soon the worship meetings were taking place once or twice a week, and his house would be full of young people.

Dr Hedayat gets on well with young people. Even now, when he is an old man, as he walks down the street he has neighbours' children running eagerly over to him, calling out, "Hello doctor – hello doctor". And in those early days it was the children who kept coming to him, wanting more 'Jesus meetings'. They specially loved the singing, and after a while they started making up their own songs in praise of Jesus. It wasn't just young children who came – some teenagers came too, and experienced God in a new way.

Dr Hedayat remembers that time very well:

Those were wonderful days. People kept bringing other people to us, and many were blessed. Lots of people came to love Jesus, especially the children.

The Holy Spirit was coming on us in very special ways. Even the small children would have visions and share messages from God. I always wrote down the visions, so we would remember what the Lord had said.

For several months these special things happened every time we met. My wife was still with us then, and she couldn't understand what was happening. One day our little girl Afsaneh told her mother that the Lord had spoken to her, and she'd seen visions of certain people coming to Jesus. Her mother didn't know what to think – but later those people DID come to Jesus.

Many people have fond memories of those days. One is an Armenian girl called Sarah, who was a teenager at that time. She recalls:

My sister was a school friend of one of Dr Hedayat's daughters, and went to meetings in his home. She became a 'real' Christian there, then gave me a Bible. I read it at home, became sure it was true, and gave my life to Jesus.

My sister saw a change in me, and guessed that something had happened. She told Dr Hedayat about it, and he invited me to come to the next meeting, as some leaders were coming from the Tehran church that week. When I went to that meeting, I told everyone that I had become a 'real' Christian. It was the first time I had done it openly. Almost at once I sensed the presence of the Holy Spirit in a new way, and I went on from there…

One day we were praying together in one of those meetings, when I had a strange and vivid vision. I felt as if I was taken up into the air. The floor felt empty under my feet, and the room around me disappeared. I seemed to be up in the sky, and I was looking down at the planet earth. It was all in dirty smoke and fire, and looked horrible. Yet when I looked around me, I was in a most beautiful place.

Everything you could imagine that is lovely, all that you dream of, was there. Then something started to push me very forcefully down towards the earth. I didn't want to go, but I was being pushed down and a voice told me, 'You must go back. I have work for you to do there.'

Sarah was to face some very difficult situations later in her life, but she has remained a wonderful witness to Christ, and her faith has been an inspiration to many people.

In the years that followed, Dr Hedayat's home became established as a centre for Christian worship and witness. He led the group, but church leaders also came from Tehran, to give Bible teaching and administer Holy Communion. People continued to invite others along, and they grew in their love for Jesus and each other. A new church had been born.

The seed had grown into a tall tree and was bearing fruit – but there were storm clouds on the horizon ...

Chapter Three

Trials and testings

IN THE SUMMER OF 1970, DR HEDAYAT HAD BEEN the only Christian in his family, and there was no church in his town. Yet in the following eight years all his immediate family had become followers of Christ, and a church was established in his home.

Then in 1979 the Islamic Revolution swept through Iran.

The year leading up to the revolution was a stressful time for everyone in Iran. The pro-Western Shah (Mohammed Reza) and his army were still in control, supported by the notoriously unpopular secret police. But the rumblings of revolution were getting louder The radical Muslim leader – Ayatollah Khomeini, was rapidly gaining popularity and the Shah – a very liberal Muslim, was rapidly losing it.

Khomeini was in exile in France at this time, but cassette tapes of his sermons were being smuggled into the country and passed around. This was done secretly at first, but later the tapes were played openly in public places. His teaching was very powerful, and called people back to a much purer form of Islam.

People started to react very strongly against anything that was not strictly Islamic. They burnt down banks as these charged interest (which is against the laws of Islam). They closed and burnt cinemas, as a lot of films were considered to be immoral. Casinos and dancing halls were all closed. Shops that sold alcohol were ransacked. Pictures of the Shah came down from people's walls, and huge posters of Khomeini went up.

Finally in early 1979, the Shah realised his cause was lost. He and his family left the country, and Ayatollah Khomeini was welcomed at Tehran airport by an estimated crowd of a million. The whole of Iranian society changed – almost overnight. The 'Glorious Islamic Revolution' had arrived.

Most Iranians welcomed the revolution, as they had a genuine desire to free their country of Western influence, and make it more God-fearing. But in the new wave of enthusiasm to establish a pure Islamic country, non-Muslims such as Christians, Jews and Bahais were viewed with great suspicion. So were liberal Muslims who led more 'Western' lifestyles. Everything associated with the Shah and the West was now seen in an extremely negative light.

In Ghazvin the Hedayat family was immediately targeted by the new regime. For not only were they known as Christians, they had Western friends and they were rich. Dr Hedayat owned a lot of land, as well as his house and X-ray clinic. Some of the land had shops on it, which brought in extra income. People were jealous, and soon most of the doctor's properties, including his clinic, were confiscated. It was not Iran's official policy to do such things, but some people used the revolution as an excuse to profiteer.

When his land was confiscated, Dr Hedayat talked to God about it. This is what he felt God was telling him:

> It is not these people who are taking your property — *I am.* For I want you to know that without all these houses, without this wealth, I can still look after you ... Don't try to get your property back ... I will give it back to you later.

Everyone in Ghazvin knew what had happened. Some were sympathetic, and asked the doctor what he was going to do about it. He would reply, "I'm not going to try and make them give my land back. No, they should come to me and offer it back."

Then he would add, "God has told me I will get it back one day – without fighting for it."

Although Dr Hedayat's lands were taken away, he still had the house he lived in, and a salary from his job at the hospital. It seemed to him that God blessed his salary, and made it cover all that he and the family needed – even the big expense of family weddings that were to come later.‡

His friends were amazed at his attitude. Sarah (the Armenian girl who had the vision of a dark smoky earth) still remembers how cheerful and positive he was.

He always had a smile on his face – it was very refreshing. They had taken his property but he took it very peacefully – he didn't get bitter and upset at all. Dr Hedayat laughed easily and was full of joy, whatever happened to him.

At around that same time, Dr Hedayat was ordered to close down his house church, and stop having any Christian meetings in his home. The authorities had noticed what was happening there, and considered it very offensive.

The doctor told his people the meetings would have to stop – but he knew that no legislation could take away what had happened in their hearts. They had come to know Jesus as their Saviour, and their faith in Him was not dependent on going to meetings. However, Dr Hedayat was still very concerned for them – they were his spiritual children. He would visit them, pray for them, laugh with them. And he would encourage them with stories of what God was doing in his life, like this one:

‡   All his children found marriage partners who shared their faith in Jesus.

One day I was in a bus, going from Tehran back to Ghazvin. I always pray for my fellow travellers, and this time I focused my prayers on a man sitting some distance in front of me. After a while that man got up. He looked all around the bus, then came and sat next to me. I laughed to myself and thought, 'maybe there's a bad smell in the place where he was before.'

After a few minutes, I started to talk with the man. Then he told me, 'When I was sitting over there, I thought I heard someone telling me to get up, and to come and sit here with you.'

The man had no idea who had told him to change places, but I knew it was the Spirit of God. So I told him my testimony, and all about Jesus. The journey from Tehran to Ghazvin is quite long so I had plenty of time!

I tell you – when we are filled with the Spirit and listening to God's voice, all sorts of things can happen.

In the following years, most of Dr Hedayat's church members kept their faith in Jesus, but some drifted away. There was even a danger with his own son Manouchehr, that when he went away to university in Tehran, he would be attracted to other ways of life. Manouchehr had many communist friends – like his father had had so many years earlier. They tried to convince him of their ideologies, but their arguments only challenged the young man to study his faith more deeply, so he could answer their questions in a more informed way. Manouchehr is now one of the few Iranians to have a PhD in Christian Theology.

All Dr Hedayat's children eventually went to Tehran to study, and he would often stay with them there. But he continued to live most of the time in Ghazvin, where he worked at the local hospital and was part of the local community. He didn't think much about his lost lands and property – he was managing very well without them.

The tree had been buffeted by the storm, but had stood firm.

The years went by, and one day in 1991 when Dr Hedayat was in Tehran, some people from Ghazvin turned up, saying they were looking for a Dr Hedayat and his son Manouchehr. When they eventually found them they said, "You can have your land and houses back now. Why didn't you try and get them back before?"

The visit of these men did not surprise the doctor, as he'd always believed he would get his property back one day. But other people were astounded. One man came to him and said: "I remember when your land was confiscated, years ago. You always said they would give it back to you one day. Now it has happened – just as you said."

Dr Hedayat was delighted to get his land back – not so much for the income it would bring, but for the knowledge that God's promise had come true.

Dr Hedayat's positive attitude to life was a great encouragement to many people. They saw the way he lived – through the problems as well as the joys of life, and it was an inspiration to them. He wasn't perfect – not by any means. But it was largely due to his cheerful example of utter commitment to Jesus, that many people in Ghazvin came to faith – and kept that faith. When the Christian meetings were stopped in their town, they weren't able to express that faith very openly – but recently something happened to change this.

Some people from Tehran were visiting a town fairly near Ghazvin, when they noticed an old church building. No one was worshipping there any more, and it was being used as a warehouse. It was damp, derelict, and depressing, but the visitors from Tehran thought of the Ghazvin Christians and wondered if they would like to use the place.

After many discussions and negotiations, the project began. People from the Tehran church joined with Dr Hedayat and others from Ghazvin, and they began to renovate that old building. There was a lot to be done in repairs, decorating and painting – but finally it was finished. When people saw the difference, they were amazed. The place that had been so run down, now looked beautiful. The church that had died in its witness, had now received a new lease of life.

Soon that church became a new outlet for worship and witness in that area of Iran. About half of its congregation are people who first came to know Jesus in Dr Hedayat's home. They are not the sum total of Dr Hedayat's spiritual children. There are people scattered all over the world, who came to know Jesus through his witness. Many are actively involved in Christian ministry.

Seeds from the tree have blown far and wide, and are bearing fruit in new places.

It is now many years since a girl had a dream, and a man with white hair told her to call her son Hedayat. But Dr Hedayat has never forgotten that dream. He believes the white-haired man was Jesus, whose 'head and hair were white as snow' (Revelation 1:14). He is sure Jesus wanted him to be called Hedayat for it means 'someone who is guided' and 'someone who guides others'.

Once there was:

- a young wife, puzzling over a strange dream
- a small child in hospital, looking at pictures of Jesus

- a curious student, listening to a man in church
- a father, taking his children out at night to show them the stars
- an unhappy man in a street, people crossing the road to avoid him
- a doctor walking across a hospital yard – meeting two men with books
- a joyful man in a living room, surrounded by children singing praise songs
- a traveller on a bus, telling the man next to him about Jesus

As Dr Hedayat thinks back over all that has happened in his life, he exclaims,

> God is in control, not man. It is not the governments that rule countries – it is Jesus Christ.

> He is King of Kings – He reigns in every situation.

> O Lord, thank you Jesus.

> O God, You have been so good to my family and me.

> You have done so much for us… we can never say it all.

The whole world cannot contain all that
You have done.

We praise You ... Alleluya.

Reflections

Dr Hedayat is an extraordinary man. Not every seed planted in Ghazvin would have grown into such a strong tree, and many pages could be written about why his life has had such an impact. There is his deep faith, his great joy in life, his lively interest in all that's going on around him, his friendships with people of all ages, his never-ending enthusiasm to talk about his Lord. All these things are very powerful.

But it is probably his prayer life that impresses people most. He is aware of the struggles that go on in people's lives, and how serious these can be. He will meet new people, ask them all about themselves, then pray for them with great sincerity – all within the first fifteen minutes of their meeting. He always brings Jesus into his conversations, and prayer seems as natural to him as breathing.

Some people see him as a legend in his own time, but like all human beings he has his faults and doesn't have all the right answers. To him, Christianity is not so much a set theology, as a minute to minute relationship with Jesus Christ.

For most of his life, Dr Hedayat has enjoyed good health, but a few years ago he had a heart attack. After talking about how God healed him, he said:

> I don't know how much longer I may have on this earth, but the apostle Paul says 'for me to live is Christ, to die is gain', and I can say the same. It will be so wonderful to be with Christ in heaven, but while we are still on earth – it too is wonderful but it is a trial. We are being tested all the time and any one of us can turn away from the Lord – even the best of us. No one can be sure they will never sin. I was fasting and praying for the last two days, in preparation for telling my story. I believe the Lord wanted me to share it, but I felt under great attack from the devil, and struggled with all sorts of temptations.

> Sometimes people think I am very experienced in my spiritual life, and that all my prayers are answered at once. But it's not like that. It's not easy for me – it's not easy for anyone. We are in a battle till the very end of our lives. None of us can glory in ourselves, or in any other human being. We can only glory in Jesus Christ. He only is worthy of our worship.

> I tell you with all my heart – Jesus Christ is Lord – He has all the glory – If God opens our eyes we can see Him everywhere. He is here with us now. Thank you Jesus...

There are many more things that Dr Hedayat could have shared – but that will be for another time. It seems fitting to end with some lines from the old Persian poet Hafez. These verses, written in the beautiful city of Shiraz so long ago, express things that have been very real in the doctor's life.

> Happy news, oh heart
> Jesus' breath has come!
> From His wholesome spirit
> Wafts the fragrance of the One.
>
> Grief's burden wearied us,
> Until God sent someone,
> Whose breath, like Jesus,
> Could lighten and uplift
> That heavy load.

V

MAR ABA'S STORY

By Teymour Shaheeni

A Travelling Companion from the 6th Century

A Travelling Companion from the 6th Century

INDIVIDUAL IRANIANS HAVE BEEN TURNING TO Christ for the last two thousand years.‡ The very first church amongst them consisted mainly of converts from the state religion, Zoroastrianism, and like converts from Islam today, these Christians faced a lot of persecution. Even in those days, the official punishment for apostasy was death.

Mar Aba was a convert from Zoroastrianism and was Patriarch of the Persian Church from 540-552 CE. As a convert his life was in danger every day, and he was fully aware that the last Patriarch who had been a convert, Babowai, had been killed.

Before turning to Christ, Mar Aba had been an aristocrat who worked in the senior ranks of the empire's civil service. He had everything to gain by remaining a Zoroastrian, and everything to lose by becoming a Christian.

Tradition tells the story of his conversion in this way. One day he was travelling in his official capacity as

‡   Acts of the Apostles 2:9

secretary to the governor of the Persian province, when they came to the River Tigris. It was Mar Aba's job to make the arrangements to get everyone in the governer's party across the river. A ferry was just about to leave, but seeing the official party the ferry master waited. Mar Aba strode over to see whether he would have to commandeer the whole ferry, or whether there was room for his party.

The ferry was not very full, and Mar Aba decided his party could fit in if only one passenger was ordered off. His eyes fell on a young man and haughtily Mar Aba ordered him to leave to make room for the governor's party. With quiet graciousness the young man left, and Mar Aba's party got on the ferry.

The young man stood on the river bank, and waited. Almost as soon as the ferry started crossing the Tigris, strong winds sprang up and drove the boat back to the shore. Again the ferry master tried to get the boat away, but again the winds drove them back.

The passengers could see the young man waiting on the river bank. His presence seemed somehow to condemn them and there were mutters that the boat was being punished for the way Mar Aba had behaved. As the winds and water lashed around the boat, people began to shout out that room should be made for the young man.

The ferry master looked at the governor, who nodded. The boat returned to the river bank, and the young man was invited in. Now as the boat set sail the winds died down, and it was a calm crossing.

It had not been a good crossing for Mar Aba. But even though his reputation was wounded, and his pride had been badly hurt, he did not allow this to overwhelm him. Instead he had become very curious in the character of this gracious young man who had shown no signs of the prickly pride he was accustomed to dealing with.

So he started to ask about this surprising stranger and discovered he was a Christian Jew. This was the start of Mar Aba's turning to Christ. Later, Mar Aba became an outstanding church leader. He re-organised the church, extended theological education, raised moral standards, and worked hard for unity with all Christians. But he never forgot the lesson he had learned from his young travelling companion on the Tigris - that as the followers of Jesus imitate His qualities of humility and self-denial, it is a powerful witness to those who do not know Him.

A FINAL WORD FROM
SAM YEGHNAZAR

Director of Elam Ministries and Pastor of
the Iranian Christian Fellowship, London

WHENEVER I READ ABOUT GOD CHANGING
somebody's life I get excited. So I've been
very excited reading these stories about
Khosrow, Hessam, Afarin and Dr Hedayat.
Personally knowing and loving them, I know
their stories are true – they prove to me
again, how wonderful God is.

It's so easy to think of God as a hard man
in the sky, somebody who's very difficult to
please...

But these stories show that God is love.

Whenever we call out to Him sincerely,
He does something for us. That's what all
these people did. They called out for help,
and God answered in such a way, they knew
this was Him. It's easy to think we're so bad
that God is just longing to condemn us. This
isn't true!

He could have condemned Khosrow for
his gambling, or Hessam for his stealing, or

Dr Hedayat for his greed. *He didn't.* Instead He showed them love and rescued them. This is exactly what the Bible says about Jesus – 'God sent Jesus into the world, not to condemn the world, but that the world might be saved through Him.' (John 3:17)

It might be you're not sure about your own relationship with God, it might be you're very aware that your character isn't all it should be, it might even be you are feeling desperately unhappy like Afarin was.

I promise, if you call out to God He will meet with you. You are just as special to Him as the dear ones who have told their stories in this book. The Bible is quite clear – 'If you seek Him you will find Him – if you draw near to God, he will draw near to you.' Why don't you bow your head right now and ask God to meet you. Tell Him all that is in your heart, and tell Him you want to enjoy a new life with Him.

Or it might be you feel you're fine and have no need of God in your life.

I don't believe you.

We all have a part of our heart that is restless till we meet God. And we all know we've done things we're ashamed of. The Bible calls this sin and it separates us from enjoying God's love. If we let sin stay in our lives, it will destroy us. God doesn't want this to happen. That's why in His love He sent Jesus Christ to die for everyone's sins.

There is no need to let sin kill your soul. Why don't you too bow your head and ask God to forgive your sins and ask Jesus Christ to come into your heart.

If you have prayed I would love to hear from you and send you some books to help you in your relationship with God. Please write to me at:

Elam Ministries
'Grenville'
Grenville Rd.
Shackleford
Godalming
Surrey
GU8 6AX
England

FURTHER READING:

- *My Persian Pilgrimage,* by William Miller: William Carey Library, Pasadena
- *Design of My World,* by Bishop Hassan B. Dehqani-Tafti: Sohrab Books, Basingstoke
- *The Hard Awakening,* by Bishop Hassan B. Dehqani-Tafti: Sohrab Books, Basingstoke
- *Christ and Christianity in Persian Poetry,* by Bishop Hassan B. Dehqani-Tafti: Sohrab Books, Basingstoke
- *Daughter of Persia,* by Sattareh Farman Farmaian: Corgi Books.
- *History of Iranian Christianity,* by Robin Waterfield
- *I dared to call Him Father,* by Bilquis Sheikh: Kingsway (ISBN 0-86065-049-9)

- *History of Christianity in Asia,* by Samuel Hugh Moffett: Orbis books (ISBN 1-57075-162-5)

- *Ten Muslims Meet Christ,* by William Miller: Out of print at the time of going to press but a good read if you can find a copy.

- Readers with Internet access may wish to visit <u>www.farsinet.com</u> for a rich variety of resources and news.